EURIPIDES' MEDEA & ELECTRA

A Commentary based on the
English Translation of Philip Vellacott

John Ferguson

D0529942

Bristol Classical Press
General Editor: John H. Betts

First published in 1987 by
Bristol Classical Press
an imprint of
Gerald Duckworth & Co. Ltd
61 Frith Street
London W1D 3JL
e-mail: inquiries@duckworth-publishers.co.uk
Website: www.ducknet.co.uk

Reprinted 1990, 1992, 1993, 1995, 1998, 1999, 2001

A catalogue record for this book is available
from the British Library

ISBN 0-86292-268-2

Originally published with assistance from the Centenary Fund of the Society
for the Promotion of Hellenic Studies

Printed in Great Britain by
Booksprint

Contents

FOR MARY HOOKER

Foreword

These notes are designed to accompany Philip Vellacott's Penguin translation of *Medea* and *Electra*.

I came to Euripides young. I was enthralled by Gilbert Murray's *Euripides and his Age*. *Medea* was the first play I read in Greek. *The Women of Troy* was the first Greek play I saw staged, in Murray's mellifluous version, with Sybil Thorndike and Margaret Rawlings. Later I saw Sybil Thorndike as a tigerish Medea with Abraham Sofaer a brilliantly subtle Jason. I read all the plays as an undergraduate, and was excited by the poetry, lucidity and iconoclasm. The comparison with Shaw (though he lacked the poetry and substituted wit) was not inept. Later, as Professor of Classics in the University of Minnesota I had the chance of working through most of the plays with a highly distinguished group of graduate students, from whom I learned much. In particular, this was during the Vietnam War, and the students had a heightened awareness of the background of the Peloponnesian War. Out of this re-examination emerged my book *A Companion to Greek Tragedy*, in which I tried to take into account the political and social background, the conditions of production, and textual detail in sometimes provocative interpretations. I have naturally recurred to some of the material there.

Equally, I have made full use of the standard editions of the Greek by D.L. Page for *Medea* and J.D. Denniston for *Electra*, though these seem more concerned with textual and grammatical matters (a necessary basis for right understanding) than with literary and dramatic values.

Finally I acknowledge two great debts of gratitude. The first to Mary Hooker, who allowed herself to be used as a guinea-pig, and to whose thoughtful and constructive comments on the first draft all users have cause to be grateful. The second to Lesley Roff, who has as ever coped skilfully with the reduction of chaotic handwriting to an ordered typescript.

John Ferguson
Selly Park

1

Introduction

1. Greek Tragedy

The origins of Greek tragedy (lit. 'goat-song') are controversial. By tradition about 534 B.C. at Athens Thespis won the prize of a goat in a competition. His originality seems to have been that alongside a chorus which danced and sang he introduced an actor or 'answerer' *(hypocrites).*

Tragedy was performed at the Spring festival of Dionysus, god of wild nature, wine and ecstasy. The philosopher Aristotle tells us that tragedy derived out of the dithyramb, the choral song in the god's honour. There is no good reason to doubt that this was one element, though not the only one.

A spring festival naturally is associated with the rebirth of the year, and Gilbert Murray tried to derive both tragedy and comedy from the idea of the Old Year killed by the murderer Winter and avenged by the New Year - essentially the pattern of the Orestes-legend used in *Electra.* This will not do as a general explanation, though our urban culture tends to forget how important fertility and the year-cycle are to an agricultural people. But it does help to explain such elements as the contest *(agon),* the sacrificial death, the messenger's speech, the lamentation, the recognition-scene, the theophany.

A third clue lies in the fact that the performers were masked. Over much of the world, in West Africa for instance, a masked dance-drama represents the presence of the ancestors. The themes of tragedy are for the most part derived from the heroic age of the ancestors, though the heroes are not confined to Athens. The word for actor *(hypocrites)* comes from a word whose earliest use is associated with interpreting the spirit-world. There was a spring ancestral festival at Athens, with Dionysus presiding. No masked dances are linked with it, but it is possible that they were transferred to the other spring festival of Dionysus: we know that at Sicyon 'tragic dances' in honour of the hero Adrastus were transferred to the service of the god.

3

Finally, we should not forget that at Eleusis near Athens there was some reenactment of the myth of Demeter and her daughter, Persephone, the Maiden. While this was a closely guarded mystery it may have influenced other religious ritual.

The origin of Greek tragedy was complex. By the fifth century there was a festival pattern by which three dramatists had a day each to present four plays *(tetralogy)*, the first three tragedies *(trilogy)*, perhaps sequential episodes in a single saga, none very long in performance, followed by a rumbustious obscene satyr-play, taking off some idea from the previous sequence. The chorus sang and danced. They were originally 50 in number, later divided into 12 for each play, giving interesting dance patterns of 3 x 4 or 2 x 6, later again increased to 15 for each play. The chorus normally enter and sometimes exeunt in anapaests, in 4/4 time (♩♩♩), a walking movement perhaps with a slight skip. The choral lyrics are in more elaborate metres. They consist of a succession of pairs of rhythmically matching stanzas, known as *strophe* (winding) and *antistrophe* (unwinding). It is reasonable to think that these constituted a dance movement (accompanying the song) round the orchestra in one direction, repeated in the reverse direction. There is usually a final stanza or *epode* delivered facing the spectators. Thespis' original actor became two, then three. (It is arguable that Sophocles *Oedipus at Colonus* requires four actors.) The actors were all male; they were trained to be athletic, and to sing and dance as well as to speak rhetorically. The fact that they were masked made it easy for a single actor to play more than one role. The leading actor was called the protagonist: it is a solecism to speak of two protagonists in a single drama.

The festival was competitive. We do not know on what grounds the judges came to a verdict, but we must not forget that the verdict was given on a sequence of four plays (not on a single play), as performed on a particular occasion, with music and choreography which we have lost.

Virtually all surviving tragedies date from the fifth century B.C. and are the work of three towering geniuses, Aeschylus, Sophocles and Euripides; yet others sometimes won the verdict. It is astonishing that a single small city, with a population not much over a quarter of a million at most, should have produced three such playwrights within a single century.

2. The Theatre

Plays were originally produced (it seems) in an improvised arena in the agora or city-centre, but a disastrous seating-collapse led to a new theatre early in the fifth century on the south side of the Acropolis by the temple of Dionysus.

The centre of this was the *orchestra,* a great dancing-floor some sixty feet in diameter with the altar of Dionysus in the middle. To the south was the stage-building, which served as a backcloth and greenroom, originally improvised, but by about mid-century permanent. The orchestra is fitted into the lower slopes of the hill, so that the spectators were clustered to the west, north and east of the orchestra, mostly looking down on it. The seating, probably originally improvised, was made permanent and of stone. (Presumably spectators brought cushions.) Stairways divided the auditorium into wedge-shaped sections, and there were lateral gangways also. It was sixty feet from the stage building to the nearest spectators, three hundred feet to the back. Yet the acoustics would be excellent for all the 14,000 capacity. Gestures would have to be broad and sweeping, and facial expression would scarcely have been visible even without masks.

The evidence is for a low stage: it is portrayed in a painting of about 420, and actors 'go up' after entry. The stage-building would represent a palace or temple, occasionally a cottage or cave which would have to be suggested by symbolic thatch or skins. The roof was sometimes used by actors, as by the watchman at the beginning of Aeschylus *Agamemnon.* There was, it seems, an elevated part of the roof used for the appearance of the gods *(theologeion)* as at the end of *Electra.* There was little or no scenery. When the chorus in Euripides *Ion* describes the scenery at Delphi it is precisely because it is *not* there for the audience to see. But we are told that Sophocles introduced scene-painting. It is not clear what this means. It might have been wooden boards in front of the *theologeion* giving the distant view. Later, three-sided structures at the side of the stage were used to indicate scenery.

Two more technical devices must be mentioned. The *mechane* or crane could be used to hoist actors in the air so that they appeared from behind the stage-building; it was used for Medea's final escape. The *ekkyklema* was probably a wheeled platform, which could be pushed out through the great central doors with a tableau

5

displayed on it: it was probably used for the appearance of the dead Clytemnestra and Aegisthus in *Electra*.

We should remember two things about the audience. The first is that this was a religious festival, but this does not imply a solemn silence or 'churchy' atmosphere. The second is that we are dealing with a highly volatile Mediterranean people, liable to burst suddenly into tears or laughter, audible and active in approbation (shouts and clapping) or disapproval (hissing, stamping and throwing fruit). Those who were merely bored ate their fruit in silence. They were critical, and had retentive memories in a predominantly oral culture, so that the comic dramatist Aristophanes could make capital out of detailed parodies. There was a small charge for admission, paid for the poorest out of public funds. Women were apparently present, as we are told that the appearance of the Furies in Aeschylus brought on miscarriages.

3. *Euripides*
Euripides was the youngest of the three great tragedians, born in 480, the product of a different age from Aeschylus (525-456) or Sophocles (496-406), post-war, more radical, more questioning, more iconoclastic. His parents were respectable tradespeople, perhaps growing and selling the produce of a farm on Salamis. His father wanted him to be an athlete, but he loathed the cult of games. He turned to painting as a profession, but at 18 was writing plays, and was only 24 when his plays were first accepted for performance in 455, though he only won third prize. We are aware of 92 plays, or 23 tetralogies. He was more popular with the people than with the official judges, and won first prize five times only, one of those posthumous.

Euripides was an innovator. He substituted romantic plays such as Alcestis, or perhaps plays full of sick humour such as *Orestes* for the rumbustious satyr-plays. He introduced a low realism of characters clothed in rags, and psychological realism of characters in rags, like Jason. He was interested in abnormal psychology (Medea and Electra are examples). He was charged with misogyny, because of his portrayal of great criminal women, but he portrayed others who are unaffectedly good, Alcestis, or Macaria in *Heracles' Children,* or Iphigeneia in *Iphigeneia in Aulis*. He understood those who are weak rather than wicked, Creon in

6

Medea, and perhaps Clytemnestra in *Electra.*

He brought to the theatre clarity of language, a strong sense of theatre, rhetorical debates (as between Jason and Medea, or Clytemnestra and Electra), brilliant messenger's speeches, exquisite song, and spectacular presentation (witness the final scene of *Medea*). He was a dramatist of ideas, rejecting the established gods and their ministers, but not the religious view of life. He was on the side of the underdog, and saw things from the standpoint of an alien, a woman, a slave, a peasant.

His life is his plays. He passed his time on Salamis in a cave with two openings and a vista; it will have been more comfortable than many houses. He had few friends. 'I have skill' says his Medea. 'Some are jealous of me; others think me unsociable.'

Then something broke within him, and he left Athens, first for Magnesia in Asia Minor, then for the court of Archelaus at Macedon, where he found the exiled historian Thucydides, the dramatist Agathon, the musician Timotheus, the painter Zeuxis. It was a wild country, where a man was not a man until he had killed his boar, and where and old man out walking might be torn to death by hounds. Here in the winter of 407-6 he died, and among his effects were found the unfinished but powerful and beautiful *Iphigeneia in Aulis,* the melodramatic *Alcmaeon at Corinth*; and one of his acknowledged masterpieces *The Bacchae.* They were presented posthumously in Athens and won first prize.

Ten of his plays survived in the general curriculum together with seven by Aeschylus and seven by Sophocles. In addition nine others were preserved by accident from some library. All except *Alcestis* date from the last twenty-five years of his life, and were written under the shadow of the great war with Sparta.

Browning in *Bishop Bloughram's Apology* paid him a tribute:

> Just when we are safest, there's a sunset touch,
> A fancy from a flower-bell, someone's death,
> A chorus-ending from Euripides, -
> And that's enough for fifty hopes and fears
> As old and new at once as nature's self.

On 22 November 1831 Goethe wrote: 'Have all the nations of the world since his time produced one dramatist who was worthy to

7

hand him his slippers?'

4. *Political Background*

Athens was a radical democracy, practising direct government by the full body of citizens (adult, male and born of Athenian parents on both sides); these may have numbered a little over 40,000 in 431 B.C. Decisions lay with the Assembly, and all citizens had the right to attend, and received pay in compensation for loss of work. The business was prepared by the Council, 500 in number, chosen by lot from the citizen-body, and serving in committees of 50 each for one-tenth of the year. Most officials were chosen by lot, though a few priesthoods were hereditary, and the 10 generals were elected for one year at a time. All office-holders were subject to scrutiny by the people's court at the end of the year. In addition, a curious device known as ostracism made possible the banishment of a politician who seemed to be getting too powerful, for ten years without loss of property or rights. (No Greek would call Britain a democracy; they would term it an elective oligarchy.)

But Athens had become an imperial power. In preparation for the great war with Persia she had built a navy, which was instrumental in winning the battle of Salamis in 480. When the war was carried across the Aegean, Sparta, a strong, conservative land-power, soon withdrew, and left Athens as leading state in the Confederacy of Delos, originally a free alliance against Persia, which developed into an Athenian empire.

Trade prospered, as Athens kept the peace of the seas. The main exports were olive oil, wine, wool and pottery, the main imports food, manufactured goods and slaves.

There was conflict with Sparta and her allies in the middle of the century. Sparta was jealous of the challenge to her predominance, Corinth of the challege to her trade. In 431 war broke out between Athens and her allies and Sparta and her allies, and dragged on, hot or cold, for 27 years. The leading Athenian statesman, Pericles, recommended withdrawing from the farms of Attica behind the strong walls of the city, and relying on imported food. Overcrowding in the city led to pestilence, from which he himself died. Then the Athenians overreached themselves in an imperialistic enterprise in Sicily (415-413) and lost two armies. They fought back with amazing resilience, but, after missing a

8

chance of an honourable peace, succumbed to disastrous defeat in 404 which Euripides did not live to see.

These events form the backcloth to the plays.

5. *Social Background*

Athens, like the rest of the world at the time, was a slave society. It has been reckoned that there may have been 110,000 slaves in a total population of about 300,000 in 431. But we must not think of the plantation slavery of the southern United States, or of Rome. The most wretched of slaves were those in the mining industry, the silver-mines at Laurium. Some slaves were public servants, police for example, or clerks. The majority were domestics, and might have considerable responsibility in looking after the children. It is not true that slaves did all the work: on the acropolis buildings slaves and free men were working side by side. All slaves were aliens, captured, bought, or bred within the home. The institution of slavery should not be defended, but it was universally practised.

Athens insisted that citizens must be born of true-blue Athenian parents on both sides. This meant that there was a considerable number of free residents without citizen-rights. They were technically called *metics*. Their number has been estimated at 25-30,000 in 431, about a tenth of the whole.

The Greeks in general, though divided from one another politically, saw themselves as superior to foreigners or 'barbarians', who went 'bar-bar-bar' instead of speaking lucid Greek. This sense of superiority underlies *Medea* and Euripides challenged it.

Athenian society was itself divided in a number of ways. Political power had at one time had a wealth-qualification. Radical democracy had done away with that, but political leadership lay for the most part with the upper classes, and right-wing politicians worked for the limitation of power to the wealthy. Aristotle saw wealth as the real divisive factor. He said that democracy was government by the poor, oligarchy by the rich, and government by a rich majority would still be oligarchy (lit., government by the few).

Within the citizen body women had no political rights. This was virtually universal until the end of the nineteenth century A.D., and changes have been more theoretical than practical in terms of

9

political power. But Athens differed from Sparta in according women far less social freedom. There has been some controversy about exactly what that meant. In general, the attitude was that women's place was in the home, where they had full reponsibility. The statesman Pericles is recorded as saying that a woman's greatest glory was not to be talked about by males for good or ill. The Athenian woman would marry very young, immediately on puberty, and her husband (always in an arranged marriage) would be much older than she. Some, no doubt, took an intelligent interest in public affairs, and influenced their husbands unobtrusively. In general the picture is not dissimilar from the Victorian age, with the husbands often loving, protective and sometimes patronizing. This attitude to women is challenged by *Medea* and *Electra*.

Education was basically simple. The pupils started the day with gymnastics, went on to music, and finished with reading, writing and arithmetic, together with the learning of poetry, thought to be morally improving, off by heart. After this elementary education there was a gap, filled during the years after the Persian War by itinerant experts known as sophists, who offered, for a fee, training for more effective participation in civil and political life. At the same time the sophists played their part in the loosening of traditional values. They tended to freedom of thought. One of the ablest, Protagoras, said that man is the measure of all things, the existence of the things that exist, and the non-existence of those that do not. This was taken to mean that if I think a thing right, it becomes right for me. In different ways Socrates and Euripides were products of this same subverting mood.

6. Medea: Date and Production
Medea is the earliest surviving tragedy by Euripides. Only *Alcestis,* a romantic substitute for a satyr-play, is earlier. It was presented in 431 as the first play in a lost sequence which included *Philoctetes* (a strong play about the wounded and abandoned hero), *Dictys* (a play about Danae and Perseus, of no great reputation), and the satyric *The Reapers* (totally forgotten). They have no obvious common theme. The judges placed Euripides at the bottom. Later tradition attributed this to the transference of the guilt of child-murder to Medea from the people of Corinth (at the

10

outset of a war partially instigated by Corinth). More likely, the verdict was affected by the weakness of two of the plays; possibly the defence of the barbarian woman and the violence of her revenge proved offensive. We are told that the play was plagiarized from one Neophron, a shadowy figure. The fragments attributed to Neophron's play are certainly later, but the authentic Neophron did introduce tutors and other slaves, and it is possible that the opening scene was suggested by something in Neophron. Also, although the play is in no sense archaic, it consists of confrontations between two actors; there are never three actors on stage together. But in general the suggestion of plagiarism is ludicrous.

7. Medea: The Legend of Argo

The background legend is one of the stories of epic heroism, itself perhaps a folk memory of the ancient journeys of the Minyans - the voyage of Jason and the Argonauts from Greece through the dangerous 'Clashing Rocks' to the eastern coast of the Black Sea, to secure the Golden Fleece, the fleece of the ram which had rescued Phrixus and Helle and taken Phrixus miraculously to Colchis, after Helle had fallen into the Hellespont and drowned. This was probably a memory of catching gold-dust in the river on a fleece. In Colchis the witch-princess Medea fell in love with the adventurer, and by her magic helped him to yoke the fire-breathing bulls, overcome the soldiers who sprang from the sowing of a dragon's teeth, and kill the snake which guarded the Fleece, and to escape, killing her brother Apsyrtus as a means of delaying the pursuit. The dowry she brought was the Fleece, the betrayal of her father Aeetes and the murder of her brother.

At Iolcus, where Jason was the rightful heir, she secured the death of his usurping uncle, but this led to their exile to Corinth. Here the traditions diverge. In one Medea was the legitimate queen of Corinth and made Jason king. Hera, in thanks to her for rebuffing advances from Zeus, had promised her children immortality. But some mishap occurred and they died.

In another version Creon was king of Corinth and offended Medea. She killed him and escaped to Athens. The people of Corinth took vengeance on her children and killed them within Hera's temple.

11

Another version told of a princess named Glauce, who to counteract Medea's poison jumped into a well later named after her.

In other words Euripides had a choice of traditions, and added his own variants. In particular, though Jason was in the traditions dependent on Medea, he never appears an anti-hero before Euripides.

8. Medea: the Characters

Medea is poetically of the highest quality and powerful dramatically, but it depends upon the characterization.

Everyone is realistically portrayed: the homely nurse; the worldly wise, self-important tutor; Creon, the weak man who likes to think himself strong; the egotistical but not unkindly Aegeus; the horrified messenger. But it is Jason and Medea who hold the stage.

Jason is a brilliant study in unfulfilled promise, resting on the achievement of the *Argo,* and gone to seed, the adventurer seeking security, the romantic lover seeking a *mariage de convenance,* the husband who has lived with his wife for years and not begun to know her. Jason is detestable - and uncomfortably like us.

By contrast, Medea, except that she is intensely a person in her own right, might be called Eros (love) incarnate, and because Love and Hate are closely allied, she has become Hate incarnate. Jason is the whole of her life - she says it twice (227,247) - for him she has betrayed her parents, killed her brother, exiled herself from her home, and made every effort to come to terms with these superior, self-satisfied Greeks. Her mother-love is real, but it is secondary to her love - and hate - for Jason. Hers is a love which must serve or destroy. It is a mighty portrayal.

9. Medea: the Dramatic Structure

The play is carefully planned, structured round three confrontations between Medea and Jason:

> 1-130 Prologue: Nurse and Tutor: Medea
> within
> 131-212 Entry of Chorus: Nurse on stage:
> Medea within

12

Two themes permeate the whole play. One is the theme of children and childlessness. This is why the scene with Aegeus is pivotal. In that scene emerges the promise that Aegeus will pass from childlessness to parenthood and the certainty that Jason will pass from parenthood to childlessness.

The other is the Argo motif, and continual use of similes and metaphor from the sea. This is the theme of high heroic endeavour - in the past. It sounds in the Nurse's first words, and is still recurring in the final scene (1335, 1385).

These images hold the play together.

10. *Medea in Art, Drama and Music*

Scenes from the story of Medea and Jason, not always precisely conforming to Euripides, appear on a number of ancient Greek vases, of which the most famous is in Munich and shows the death of the princess, the murder of the children, and the escape in the sun-chariot. We know that Timomachus, an artist of the first century B.C., made a famous painting of Medea, divided between hatred of Jason and love of the children, with 'tears in her menace, anger in her compassion'. A wall-painting in Herculaneum may be a copy of this. Medea and the children also appear in Pompeii in the Casa dei Dioscuri, but the conception and execution are sadly inferior. Much the most powerful modern version is by Delacroix (1798-1863) in the Louvre, with versions in Lille and Berlin.

13

Medea, her hair flying, her breasts bare, sits in a dramatic landscape, looking over her right shoulder to where vengeance is pursuing her: she holds a sword in her left hand and with her right arm grips the chilren to prevent their escape. She is 'outwardly calm but with all the passion of despair' wrote Walter Friedlaender, who regarded this as the culmination of the painter's achievement.

The Spanish Roman Seneca (4 B.C.-A.D. 65) wrote a play *Medea,* perhaps for rhetorical declamation rather than stage performance. He turned tragedy into melodrama by emphasizing Medea's savagery and playing down Jason's faults, and by a scene of witchcraft. The play contains some brilliant epigrams, not least Jason's final words:

Go on through the vast heights of the towering sky
and testify that where you pass there are no gods.

Some modern dramatists have taken up the theme, notably the French Jean Anouilh (1946) who used mythology to reflect the present: his Medea is powerful but a shade shrill and overdrawn. He is closer to Seneca than Euripides. The American Robinson Jeffers (1887-1962) was too self-conscious in his psychological analysis of the characters. Maxwell Anderson (1888-1959) was more successful in *The Wingless Victory,* in which he took the theme and adapted it to the modern U.S.A.

The finest operatic treatment was by Luigi Cherubini (1760-1842), an Italian who settled in Paris. *Medea* was his fourth French opera, and his finest. Medea is an exacting dramatic role. The orchestra has reduced percussion and no trumpets, and this increases the tragic intensity. Expressive vocal writing is matched by symphonic orchestration, and Medea's role is unified, and not a series of isolated arias. The neglect of this work is astonishing: Callas revived it in 1953.

Iannis Xenakis, a Rumanian-born Greek, and a contemporary, is a highly mathematical composer. He wrote music for a version of Seneca's *Medea* (1967). The suite from it is stark in the extreme, but not impersonal and not without power: the play may be Seneca's but Xenakis cannot get Euripides out of his mind, and the contra-bassoon at the end shows Jason as a pricked bubble.

11. *Electra: Date and Production*

There is a question-mark against the date of production of *Electra*. Stylistic considerations place it between *Andromache* (c. 420) and *The Women of Troy* (415) and suggest that it was written 419-416. But the words of the Dioscuri about a naval expedition to Sicily (1347-8) must refer to the relief expedition for the Athenian forces in Sicily in 413. We know very little about the way in which Athenian playwrights devised their trilogies when they were not episodes in a single drama. It is possible that Euripides wrote the bulk of the play in 419-416, but held it until he could fit it in to a suitable combination of other plays. It would fit well with *Iphigeneia among the Taurians*, which may reasonably be dated to 413, and which dealt with Agamemnon's other daughter. Further, lines 1280-3 seem related to another play *Helen*. This is usually dated to 412, because Aristophanes in *The Thesmophoriazusae* in 411 links *Andromeda* and *Helen*, saying that *Andromeda* was 'last year'. But *Helen* is only said to be 'recent', and it is just possible that *Helen*, about Clytemnestra's sister and Agamemnon's brother, was also one of the plays of 413. At the very least we must say that Euripides had it already in mind.

We have also a surviving play by Sophocles on Electra. It is a play of very different mood, brilliantly structured as drama, focussing more on the killing of Aegisthus than the matricide, portraying Electra as heroic rather than pathological. The date is quite uncertain. Stylistically it stands between *King Oedipus* (c. 429-425) and *Philoctetes* (409), which is a long span of time. It has been much argued which *Electra* came first. Wilamowitz, the great German scholar, argued strongly that Euripides wrote the earlier play. Many scholars take a different view and place Sophocles *Electra* in the early 410s. But we cannot be certain.

Both plays were written against a background of war, already long and drawn out. The theme is violence.

Forty years before, in 458, Aeschylus had presented *The Oresteia* as a trilogy. The second play, *The Libation Bearers*, deals with the same events: this is the only myth on which we have surviving plays from all the three great tragedians of Athens.

Euripides in his play alludes unfavourably to what he regards as the clumsy devices whereby Electra recognises Orestes in Aeschylus' version. All three treatments are different in tone. Sophocles seems primarily concerned with the dramatic power of the story. Aeschylus and Euripides are more obviously interested in the moral issues. But they also differ from one another. To Aeschylus the killing of mother by son in requital for his father's murder presents an acute moral dilemma narrowly resolved in the final play in Orestes' favour. Euripides has no such doubts: the matricide is a crime.

12. *Electra: the Legend*

In the background was a long ancestral myth.

Tantalus was a Lydian who became immortal by sharing in the gods' banqueting. But he offended the gods - in different ways according to different stories. He stole nectar and ambrosia; or he betrayed the gods' secrets; or he tested their omniscience by inviting them to dinner and killing and cooking his son Pelops. In the last story Demeter took a bite from the shoulder: Pelops was restored to life with an ivory shoulder; Tantalus was condemned to eternal punishment.

Pelops became a refugee in Greece. He won his bride Hippodameia in a chariot-race with her father Oenomaus, by bribing the latter's charioteer to equip the chariot with wax lynchpins so that he crashed. But Pelops then murdered the guilty charioteer, who invoked a dying curse on Pelops and his descendants.

Pelops had a large family. His best-known sons were Atreus and Thyestes, who stood under the curse. Banished by their father, they took refuge in Mycenae. Atreus had two sons, Agamemnon and Menelaus, by Aerope. But Aerope fell in love with Thyestes, and betrayed her husband by stealing from him a golden fleece and giving it to her lover. This was used to determine the succession to the throne of Mycenae. Atreus thereon murdered two of Aegisthus' sons and served them up to him in a banquet. Thyestes was thus polluted and had to go into exile. Atreus took the throne. Thyestes, in a contorted story, had an incestuous relationship with his daughter Pelopia, who bore him Aegisthus. After Atreus' death, Thyestes came back to Mycenae as king, but was ousted in turn by Agamemnon and Menelaus, and again exiled, with Aegisthus.

Leda, wife of Tyndareos, king of Sparta, was ravished by Zeus in the form of a swan, and gave birth to - or hatched out - the Dioscuri, Castor and Polydeuces (Pollux), and the two girls, Clytemnestra and Helen. Clytemnestra married Agamemnon, and bore him two daughters, Electra and Iphigeneia, and a son Orestes. Helen, the most beautiful woman in the world, married Menelaus, who succeeded Tyndareos as king of Sparta.

At the marriage of the human Peleus with the sea-goddess Thetis, gods and humans attended in profusion. But Eris, Strife, appeared uninvited and dropped a golden apple inscribed FOR THE FAIREST. Hera, goddess of Argos and consort of Zeus, Athene, goddess of Athens and of war and wisdom, and Aphrodite, goddess of Corinth and of love, contended for it. They made Paris, prince of Troy, arbiter. Each tried to bribe him, with political power, military victory, or marriage to the most beautiful woman in the world. In the romanticism of youth, he chose the last. The most beautiful woman in the world was married to Menelaus. Paris went on a deputation to Sparta, and eloped with Helen (though there was a counter-myth that she was spirited away to Egypt and Paris was fobbed off with a phantom).

The Greeks sought revenge and raised a huge fleet under the command of Agamemnon. Faced with hostile winds, he was told that he must sacrifice his daughter Iphigeneia to Artemis, whom he had offended. He brought her to Aulis, where the fleet was waiting, under the pretext of marriage to the great soldier Achilles, and sacrificed her (again there was a counter-myth that she was spirited away to the far north and a deer substituted).

Clytemnestra did not forgive the death of her daughter. The war dragged on for ten years. Aegisthus returned to Mycenae, and she accepted him as her lover. When Agamemnon returned triumphant with the Trojan princess Cassandra as spoils-of-war and his concubine, Clytemnestra, with Aegisthus' support, killed them both. Orestes, the rightful heir, was either smuggled away or already absent, and grew up with Pylades, prince of Phocis. Electra was left behind. (Her name means 'Unmarried' and it was a startling innovation of Euripides to have her married off to a peasant.)

The Delphic Oracle, whose presiding god was Apollo, told

17

Orestes that he must avenge his father. To do this, he had to kill his mother, itself a polluting act. Here lie some of the tensions of the story. What happened is variously recounted. Orestes, with the support of Pylades and Electra, killed Aegisthus and Clytemnestra, and in some versions was driven mad by his mother's avenging Furies until he could find purification.

13. Electra: the Characters

Electra in Euripides is a brilliant pathological study, fascinated and repelled by sex, with her masochism and sadism, her fixation on her father and hatred of her mother, her obsessive hopes and fears, her dominating personality.

At her side Orestes, whom she has idealized, is a spiritless coward, marked by fatal irresolution. Between the two there is a kind of Medea-Jason situation; she is powerful, he is empty.

Clytemnestra has none of the dominant qualities of Aeschylus' queenly murderess. She excites more pity than terror. She is weak, scared of public opinion. She has some concern for Electra; she expresses remorse for her crime. She is not an innocent victim but Euripides contrasts her weakness with the children who kill her.

Aegisthus does not appear. In Aeschylus he is a typical blustering dictator. In Sophocles he shows courage at the last. In Euripides, we see him through the hatred of Electra, but the reality is curiously courteous, and it is his killer who is ignoble.

Pylades does not speak; in Aeschylus his brief intervention is decisive. Here he is simply at the side of Orestes. But if Orestes is as he is, what are we to think of the company he keeps?

In all there is only one decent character, the peasant, 'the only gentleman present' (says E.B. England ironically), a breath of sanity in a world of explosive and destructive madness.

14. Electra: the Dramatic Structure

The stagebuilding represents not a palace or temple but a cottage.

1-111   Prologue, in three parts: 1-53 A Peasant to whom Electra has been married off, soliloquizes, setting the scene. 54-81

	Peasant and Electra in rags. 82-111 Orestes (with Pylades unspeaking).
112-212	A great monody by Electra, followed by a song shared between Chorus of local women and Electra.
213-431	Orestes and Pylades appear but do not reveal who they are. Long dialogue between Orestes and Electra. Peasant appears and welcomes the guests.
432-486	Choral song.
487-698	Old Servant of Agamemnon appears and identifies Orestes to Electra. The scene is broken by a brief song of joy from the Chorus (585-95). The three plan revenge: the Old Man with Orestes, then with Electra, then all three pray.
699-746	Choral song.
747-858	A Messenger arrives with news of Aegisthus' death.
859-879	A brief choral song interrupted by spoken words from Electra.
880-987	Electra makes a speech of hatred over the dead Aegisthus. They plan Clytemnestra's death, Orestes drawing back.
988-997	Brief choral song.
998-1146	Clytemnestra arrives; Orestes is inside. There is a semi-formal debate between mother and daughter, the mother gentle and reasonable, the daughter fanatical. They go in.
1147-1171	Brief choral song broken by the death-cries of Clytemnestra.
1172-1232	The bodies are brought out on the moving platform. The murderers sing, brought low by what they have done.
1233-1359	The Dioscuri, brothers of Clytemnestra, appear, and condemn the revenge, however merited, and foretell the several destinies. Brother and sister part from one another.

There are some unusual features in this structure. First there are only two full choral lyrics (432-86, 699-746), and both are filled with ugliness. The first is filled with monsters, the second turns to adultery, deceit and theft - and murder and cannibalism. More than ever we wish we had the music and choreography. Second, there is a great deal of tight *stichomythia* (line for line exchanges between the characters): 220-89 Orestes and Electra; 622-84 Old Man and Orestes, Old Man and Electra, broken by one couplet; 962-84 Orestes and Electra, broken by one couplet. The first two passages are unusually long. Third, the play centres on Electra: we see her set off by the decent, honest peasant, the weak Orestes, the bloodthirsty Old Man, the dead Aegisthus, the pitiable Clytemnestra.

There are three images of particular importance which recur through the play. One is light, and it is ambiguous. The dawn which begins the play (but Electra invokes Night), the day the chorus welcome (585), turn to darkness. The second is represented by the monsters who darken the first choral lyric and appear again later (Gorgons and Furies especially). Of less importance, but still significant, is the theme of athletic contest, suggested by Achilles in the first long choral ode, and repeated: note Electra (751) 'The fight' - literally, contest, - 'is on', the image of the runner (825), the garlands of victory.

There is plenty of spectacle: Electra in rags with a waterpot on her head; the scene of prayer; the garlanding; Clytemnestra's entry, her finery contrasting with Electra's rags; the final scene at two (or even three) levels, using *theologeion,* orchestra, and perhaps stage.

Euripides writes a powerful play. It is a play with a message. To him the murder is a crime, and he organizes the drama to stress this. He therefore attacks the god who orders the murder: Apollo - and of course his human ministers at Delphi. Alongside this he is making a defence of women. Clytemnestra denies the twofold standard of morality, different for male and female (1041). True that Electra with her father-fixation twice says that the male should rule (932, 1052), but it is she who in fact controls the action. Her authority, for good or ill, strides across the play.

Euripides criticizes the way Aeschylus, and probably Sophocles, handled the story, particularly but not solely in the recognition scene; also in setting the play away from the palace where strangers would hardly have found easy admission.

20

Euripides criticizes Apollo, but he does not let the humans off the hook: Electra anyway is not under Apollo's orders (1303). The divine epiphany at the end is no solution. Gods do not appear like this to save a situation, and Euripides makes that clear when the Dioscuri are asked why they did not intervene to save their sister, and have no real answer (1298). Nor will they intervene to save the Athenian ships and men in Sicily. Thirteenth-hour solutions, running counter to the logic of events, do not occur. It is Euripides' challenge to Athenian military imperialism, and the warring states of Greece.

15. *Electra in Art, Drama and Music*

Scenes of the vengeance of Orestes and Electra on Aegisthus and Clytemnestra are sometimes portrayed in ancient art, not necessarily with reference to a particular version of the drama. Thus the brother and sister are seen at Agamemnon's tomb in painting and terracotta. A great vase-painting from Berlin shows the death of Aegisthus. An extraordinary low-relief reproduced in Michael Grant's *Myths of the Greeks and Romans* shows Clytemnestra finding Aegisthus dead, Orestes turning, dagger in hand, and Electra flinging up her arms in exultation.

The theme has attracted some modern dramatists, who find the ancient myths a valid way of expressing themes which still ring true, because they say something fundamental about human nature. The best known is the American Eugene O'Neill's *Mourning Becomes Electra* (1931) set in nineteenth-century New England, strong on the theme of sexual repression, less strong on the religious and moral issues. Jean Giraudoux's *Electra* (1937), one of a whole series of such modernizations by French dramatists, is beautifully written. He uses a powerful symbol in a vulture high over the head of Aegisthus, gradually planing lower. His avenging Furies are girls who grow into womanhood as the deaths draw nearer. Jean-Paul Sartre in *The Flies* (1943), written with strong allusion to the German occupation of France, shows them as flies, and the polluted city of Argos similarly plagued. T.S. Eliot's *The Family Reunion* (1939) deals with the period after the murder: the Furies are felt as a shadowy presence.

By far the most powerful of these modern treatments is Richard Strauss' colossal opera to a libretto by Hugo van Hofmannsthal.

The plot is broadly that of Sophocles, but the dominant, pathological Electra, one of the most exacting of all soprano roles, is taken from Euripides.

MEDEA

Note: the numbers refer to lines in the Greek text. They appear at the top of each page in the Penguin translation, but do not correspond line by line.

1-130. *Prologue. The nurse explains what took place before the beginning of the play and prepares the ground for the action to come.*
1. The opening is noteworthy. (a) It is spoken not by a god or hero, but by a slave. (b) The first name is not Jason or Medea but Argo (introduction section 7), one of the key motifs to watch for. (c) Another key motif, the sea, is there by implication. (d) It was a commonplace of Greek moralists that there was something wrong about trying to 'conquer' the sea (sensitive Indians deplore the idea of 'conquering' Everest, saying that humans should cooperate with Nature not conquer it.) To the Greeks the sea was an ancient divine power; this came to be expressed in the figures of Poseidon and scores of other sea-gods, sea-goddesses and sea-nymphs, but the feeling was deeper than the myths. To do violence to this ancient divine power was a form of *hybris,* arrogant pride, and would meet Nemesis (retribution). (e) The words are sinister and full of foreboding. (f) The sentence is vivid and striking, with strong alliteration in the original Greek. Aristophanes in *Frogs* 1382 lets Euripides choose it as a line worth weighing against a line of Aeschylus. It was much imitated and echoed, by the Latin poets Catullus (64,171) and Vergil *(Aen.* 4,657) for instance.
2. **jaws of rock**: the Symplegades or Clashing Rocks (intr. sec. 7).
3. **Pelion**: mountain of Thessaly above Volos (the ancient Iolcus).
8. **mad with love**: Eros, Love, is a power which makes you act irrationally. Medea is governed by this mighty, irrational force. Jason is not said to be mad with love for her. Her love rejected turns to an equally passionate hatred. The love-theme is delicately treated by Apollonius of Rhodes, an epic poet of the third century B.C., who is one of our main sources for the saga.
9. **Pelias' daughters**: Medea persuaded them to rejuvenate their

23

father by killing him and boiling his remains in a cauldron. Not unnaturally, it led to his death at their hands: Medea and Jason were banished from Iolcus and took refuge in Corinth. This was the theme of one of Euripides' first plays *The Daughters of Pelias* (455 B.C.), now lost.

10. **her children**: the first mention of them. 'Her' is not in the Greek: the absence of the possessive distances them from Medea.

11. **earned**: by offering sacrifices which ended a famine.

14. **Obedience**: strong irony. This and the maxim which follows sound more like Jason's point of view - and, for that matter, the view of the average Athenian man in the audience.

16. Our first picture of Medea is through the nurse's eyes. We know she is passionate, capable of murder or bringing blessing. In the rest of the speech the picture is fleshed out.

18. **for a royal bed**: the Greek says that 'he is sleeping with a royal bed' i.e. there is no love only ambition.

19. **He has married Glauce**: Greek marriage was monogamous, and the Greeks scorned polygamy as 'barbarian'. But Greek marriage-law would hardly apply to a foreign wife such as Medea, who could well be regarded as a concubine. Further the husband could achieve divorce simply by expelling his wife, though he might be compelled to return the dowry. But why did Creon seek the marriage of his daughter to a penniless adventurer? Partly because of his heroic reputation, partly because there is a blurring of legends and in one Medea's husband is the rightful king of Corinth.

21. **vow and solemn pledge**: it was a commonplace that the Persians and other 'barbarians' cared intensely about truth-telling and oath-keeping; the Greeks did not. The Greek here speaks of the 'right hand' (used in a solemn pledge). It is important not to lose the reference, which is taken up at 496 and 899.

28. **rock or wave of the sea**: both important symbols, reminding us of the voyage.

36. **hates her sons**: the first inkling of their danger: the explicit statement is at 792.

38.**mind**: after this, five melodramatic lines, not by Euripides, but written by some later producer, are omitted.

46. **Here come the boys**: there are no stage directions in the original Greek: a line such as this serves as a stage-direction.

48. **young heads**: the nurse is characterized as sententious.

49. **Old nurse**: the tutor is another slave; he did not teach, except

incidentally, but acted as a protective escort and kept an eye on behaviour. His first words are slightly pompous and lent themselves to parody by the comic dramatist Alexis (fr. 176 K).

54. **the blow that strikes**: the Greek word is cognate with that rendered 'obedience' at 14, which adds to the irony.

57-8. **I had to come...heaven**: famous and much parodied lines. The sun sees all, avenges wrongs and drives away darkness: in this play he intervenes on Medea's side.

62. **the worst**: in the original there is some wordplay in this opening scene on the word *neos*: 37 revolutionary ('some dreadful purpose'); 48 young; 62 news.

64. **Why, nothing's happened**: typical of the shifty tutor to leak a secret, and then be secretive about it. Dramatically, the news is first withheld from the audience, then shared with the audience and withheld from Medea.

69. **Peirene**: fountain in the centre of Corinth, an obvious area to meet and gossip. Pausanias in his account of Greek geography, writing of the rebuilt Roman city, calls it 'the pride of Corinth', and says that the water was good to drink (2,3,3).

70. We note that the tutor cannot keep the news to himself for long.

79. **we're rid of**: the Greek metaphor is from baling out a ship, but regularly used with the idea of seeing something through to the end.

82. **Children**: the children are present in this scene and elsewhere as non-speaking characters.

85. **What man's not guilty?**: the tutor is cynical as well. The Greek has another line after 86, clumsy and destroying the balance of the dialogue, clearly another insertion by some maladroit editor or producer.

89. **the house**: stage direction and indication of the set.

90-5. The second inkling of danger to the children.

92. **wild bull's**: like the fire-breathing bulls of Colchis (intr. sect. 7)

96. Our direct introduction to Medea is a great wailing cry behind the scenes. The metre of the verse now changes, for the nurse as well as for Medea, from the iambics used for ordinary dialogue (♩♩) to quickened anapaests (♩♩♩).

109. **Deep in passion and unrelenting**: two words in Greek, the first a technical term from medical science, strangely placed in the

nurse's mouth, a bold effect.

113. **Death take you**: her first cry was for herself, her second a curse on Jason and the children.

119. **mind of a queen**: the Greek is stronger, a dictator or autocrat (tyrannos), not a constitutional ruler. Medea was a princess, as well as magician and wronged lover.

125. **the middle way**: sententious again. There was a famous Greek maxim, associated with Delphi, 'Avoid excess'.

131-212. *Parodos (first entry of Chorus). The chorus consists of Corinthian women who are shown to be sympathetic to Medea.*

137. **where my loyalty lies**: this reflects an old legend that Medea, through her father Aeetes, was rightful queen of Corinth: it is really loyalty to her.

138. **Jason's house? It no longer exists**: ominous words: in Medea's mind already true of both his old house and his new.

144. **Come, flame of the sky**: the thunderbolt of Zeus, god of oaths.

·148. **O Zeus, and Earth, and Light**: the beginning of a song and dance by the chorus, echoed in identical rhythm at 173 ('I wish she would') and completed at 204-12 ('I heard her'). The invocation is important. Medea makes Aegeus swear by Earth and Sun and all the gods (746-7, 752-3). The chorus as the climax approaches invokes Earth and Sun (1251-2). Jason at the end will point to Sun and Earth (1327-8) and call on Zeus (1405).

150. **wife in her anguish**: the Greek, ambiguously, says 'bride': Glauce will shortly be crying out in anguish.

160. **Themis** was goddess of social justice, protector of promises: the name is cognate with the English word Doom. Artemis is here identified with Nemesis, the fatal retributress of wrong.

167. **My brother**: Apsyrtus was Medea's young brother; he was with her on the escape from Colchis; she killed him and cut him up dropping the pieces one by one to delay the pursuers as they collected them. She is not without experience in killing children, even those close to her by blood.

169. **Zeus**: Medea has not named him but he was guardian of oaths (161).

187-8. **like a mad bull or lioness**: in Greek an exceedingly bold mixed metaphor (not simile), 'turned to a bull with a lioness' glare'. The animal symbolism is important: for the bull see on 92.

190ff. **The men of old times...**: again sententious: interesting

26

reflections (of which Plutarch approved - *Moralia* 143 D; 710 E) ending in an earthy sentiment. David played to calm Saul in his mad fits (1 *Samuel* 16,23 and Robert Browning's Dramatic Lyric 'Saul') and Achilles to quieten his own vexed spirit (Homer *The Iliad* 9,186). But music is not going to soothe Medea.

211. **the salt strait**: probably the Bosporus, possibly the Dardanelles.

213-409. *First episode: Medea and Creon. The action of the play begins here with Medea's entrance.*

214 **Women of Corinth**: in public Medea is self-possessed. Note her concern for her reputation, typical enough in a Greek male.

228. **Jason was my whole life**: the probable meaning of the Greek, and key to her actions.

230ff. **we women**: for the place of women in society see intr. sect. 5.   It is impossible to overstress the power of Euripides' imagination in this identification with the woman's viewpoint - or the disturbing effect it must have had on the males in his fifth-century audience.   Note the reference to dowry and to arranged marriages (though hers was a love-match which turned out disastrously).

233. **Possessor of our body**: still an issue in John Galsworthy's *A Man of Property*.

236. **divorce**: legally possible for the woman on the grounds of infidelity or brutality, but seldom practised.

238. **a foreign woman**: the translator's gloss, and it is certainly true that Euripides stresses Medea as underprivileged both as woman and foreigner.   But the point here is more profound: a woman *always* enters her husband's home as a stranger to its practices.   'Divine inspiration' would be a more accurate translation than 'magic' (239).

245. **he can go out**: there is a relevant verse 'Higgamus Hoggamus women are monogamous/Hoggamus Higgamus men are all polygamous.'

249-50. **they go out to battle: fools!**: an astonishing flight of the imagination on the part of Euripides and one that would not have gone down well with his Greek male audience.   Remember there were no anaesthetics.

255. **I have no city**: in Greek ears a terrible fate.   See also 644, and Sophocles *Antigone* 370.

256. **a land at the earth's edge**: 'barbarian'.   Herodotus (1,2,2)

says that she was kidnapped.

257. **brother**: this is pretty cool, when she murdered him (see on 167).

263. **Say nothing**: Horace says of the tragic chorus: 'It should conceal what is conveyed to it' (*Ars Poetica* 200).

weak and timid: a typical stereotype which patently does not apply to Medea.

269. **I see Creon**: another stage direction.

271. **You there, Medea**: Creon is a weak man, abrupt and blustering.

278. **full sail**: nautical metaphor recurring; we are reminded of the voyage of the Argo.

292ff. **My reputation...**: a famous speech. A little over two decades later Euripides, a 'clever' man in the eyes of the man in the street, was driven into voluntary exile in Macedon. Compare also the fate of Socrates, whom the Athenians sought to exile but who uncompromisingly chose death.

324. **I kneel to you**: Medea kneels to men three times in the play, each time in a calculated move to gain her purpose. The words usher in a passage of *stichomythia,* line for line conversation, of the sort Shakespeare uses in *Much Ado* and *Richard III.*

330. **what an evil power love**: yes, indeed, hers for Jason's and Jason's for Glauce.

331. Creon 'here is magnificently prosy' - Page.

342. **you are a father too**: she appeals to the very feeling with which she will do havoc.

347. The chorus revert to the anapaests (see on 96).

359. **where can you turn?**: this dramatically anticipates the arrival of Aegeus.

362. **In the sea**: the vital image again.

369. **carry out my schemes**: cf. 'in the act' (382) 'with all your skill' (402) - all the same word in Greek, all speaking of technical proficiency (in magic).

375. **and my husband**: she will change her plan; it is a worse punishment to leave him alive.

385. **To kill by poison**: the speech is filled with overtones of magic: see on 369, and the reference to Hecate (397) and the Sun (406), and the final words of the speech (409). Helios, the Sun, has the sorceress Circe for daughter and Medea for granddaughter.

390. **strong tower of help**: again anticipating Aegeus' arrival.

393. Take sword in hand: she has rejected this once, but the succession of thought is clear: 'I'll kill them with a sword...No, I would be taken in the act...Poison them...But I'll still be taken unless I have an escape route...If there is no escape I *will* use the sword: if I'm to die, better to kill with my own hand.'

396. hurt me and not suffer for it: again, to the Greeks, a male sentiment.

397. Hecate: underworld goddess, presiding over the magical arts. She appears as queen of the witches in Middleton *The Witch* or Shakespeare *Macbeth*. Note that this is the central altar in Medea's house: in Athens Hecate's altar stood outside the gates. Earlier she was more benign, and is fascinatingly evoked in Hesiod *Theogony* 411-52.

402. scheme with all your skill: a covert pun linking Medea's name with a Greek word for scheme *(medos)* for which a synonym is used. For a different word-play see on 717.

405. Sisyphus: king and in some traditions founder of Corinth, a proverbial trickster, who lived to a great age by tricking the powers of death, eventually being forced as punishment to roll a boulder uphill without ever reaching the top. In one tradition he succeeded Medea as ruler of Corinth (Pausanias 2,3,8).

406. the Sun-god: Helios, whose consort Perse or Perseis gave birth to Aeetes and the sorceress Circe; one granddaughter, Chalciope, married Phrixus (intr. sect. 7); the other was Medea.

410-445. First Stasimon or choral song.

410. Streams of the sacred rivers flow uphill: a choral song with two pairs of matching stanzas, the first pair a general meditation on woman, the second on Medea. The opening words are an adaptation of a proverbial phrase. This song with its reaffirmation of the woman's standpoint is important to the 'feel' of the play.

421. Male poets of past ages: a very modern sentiment: males control the media and create the stereotype of women. There is an extended poem by Semonides in dispraise of womankind (fragment 7), attacks on particular women by Archilochus and Hipponax, generalized sentiments in Homer *(Odyssey* 11,456 'you can't trust women these days') and Hesiod *(Works and Days* 375 'to trust a woman is to trust deceivers'), and there must have been accounts of women performing actions contrary to the dominant male ethos, and sometimes to any moral code, in lost epics.

426. Phoebus: Phoebus Apollo, whose double name betrays a complex origin, was among other things the god of lyric poetry and of the arts generally. But there were female poets in Greece: in addition to Sappho, the greatest and best-known, Corinna, Praxilla, Telesilla, Charixena, Cleobulina, Erinna, Theano of Locri, to name a few. Such freedom was not available to Athenian women, at any rate of the citizen class, though it was found in other parts of Greece.

431. **Set sail**: the nautical theme once more.

433. **Rocky Jaws**: see on 2.

439. **The grace of sworn oaths**: an unusual phrase. The stress on the oath is vital to the play.

446-626. *Second episode: Jason and Medea (1)*.

446. **I have often noticed**: the first of three confrontations between Jason and Medea. Jason enters from the audience's right (from the city, as convention ruled). Where Creon has been blustering, Jason is self-satisfied. Notice that although the audience are expecting him at some time we do not know who he is until he speaks his own name at 452: Medea cannot bring herself to speak it in this scene (note the contrast with 869 when she wants to get something out of him). The first confrontation ends in deadlock, but with Jason, on the face of it, holding all the cards.

461. **the children are not sent away with an empty purse**: he does not seem to mind them being exiled.

464. **I could never bear ill-will to you**: what a thing to say to the woman who is all passion towards him!

465. **You filthy coward!**: what follows is a near-formal debate of the type the Athenian audiences loved, with two speeches of exactly the same length. Athenian life was full of contests (Gk. *agon*, from which we derive *agony* and pro*tagonist*, the first actor in competitive drama). There were competitions in athletics, drama, music, pottery, horsebreeding, sailing. A lawsuit was a contest between orators; so were the political debates which governed the city.

476. **I saved your life**: there is a remarkable effect in the Greek with six successive syllables beginning with an 's'-sound. Medea hisses the words. Jason lives on fame (544). What is his fame except the winning of the Fleece? Medea's claim in this speech is that he owes his fame to her. For the events see intr. sect. 7. She does not mention her brother's murder.

477. **Argo**: the ship is named at key points in the play (compare 1,1335).

30

490. **childless**: the Greeks, like Africans today, placed strong value on sons as props to old age and to carry on the line, and blamed the wife for infertility or female progeny only (not knowing that the latter lies with the father).

491. **hankering after**: the Greek word, related to *eros,* means passionate love.

492. **respect for oaths**: a recurring theme: see on 21,439.

494. **new laws**: the words are curiously parallel to the comic view of the scientific revolution expressed a few years later in Aristophanes *The Clouds*: 'Zeus has been kicked out and Vortex is on the throne' (828). There too it is associated with a change of moral values. Zeus was the guardian of the oath. Ironic that Euripides should be associated in the popular mind with Socrates and the sophists (intr. sect. 5).

495. **perjury**: again the respect for oaths.

496. **My poor right hand, which you so often clasped**: a sudden, vivid personal picture. It can hardly be Medea's fantasy. Was Jason genuinely in love with Medea? Or was he using her to secure the fame of his exploit? Part of the subtlety of the play is that it is left ambiguous. But the portrayal of Jason is such that we suspect that he might not have known the difference. The words look back to 21 and forward to 899.

499-514. Note the many ironic statements in this section of Medea's speech

519. **revealing mark**: lit. the stamp which authenticates a coin.

521. **in the place of dearest love**: the chorus, whose words at this sort of point in tragedy often seem banal, here hits upon the deep springs of Medea's personality. But the word rendered 'dearest love' is not *eros,* passion, which Medea has, and which easily turns to *eris,* strife, a word which appears in the Greek here, but *philia,* mutuality of affection, which Jason and Medea, both filled with their own selves, have not enjoyed.

523. **hurricane**: Jason's nautical metaphor rings false, almost like a landlubber in a yachting-cap. At best he is living in the past, reliving the voyage.

527. **Aphrodite**: this is unlikely to endear him to Hera and Athene, the two goddesses who were the divine inspiration of his exploit, and who induced Aphrodite, goddess of love, to make Medea fall in love with Jason. He is attempting to rebut Medea's claim on his gratitude; she was not acting freely but by Aphrodite's will.

31

530. **helpless passion**: Eros, a divine, ineluctable power. Jason strikes near the bone. He cleverly admits her help without needing to feel gratitude to her.

533. Jason is being very patronizing here.

536. **left a barbarous land...Hellas**: many of the audience must have cheered. But the irony is marked. Were the Greeks civilized and the rest of the world uncivilized? Were lying, shifty, oath-breaking Greeks better than Persians to whom oaths were sacred? A century later Alexander set out to conquer Persia. He had been taught by Aristotle that non-Greeks ('barbarians') were slaves by nature (*Politics* 1,1252b9). He found Greeks who he could not trust and Persians whom he could, and came to the conclusion that the good man is the only real Greek, and the wicked man the only real barbarian (Strabo 1,4,9). We in the West have too often Jason's attitude to our 'civilization': Euripides speaks to us today. Medea does not care an obol about civilization. She does not want civilization. She wants Jason. If he showed an atom of real love for her, her passionate hatred might still turn back to passionate love. But he prates of civilization and cool self-interest. It is told of both Socrates and Plato that they regularly thanked God that they were born Greek not 'barbarian', male not female, free not slave. This play challenges two of those assumptions: Euripides challenged the third in his lost play *Alexander*.

540. **You are famous**: Jason is expressing his own values, but Medea also cares for reputation. But note the assumption that fame is confined to Greece.

543. **Orpheus**: a semi-divine figure from Thrace, whose singing charmed the wild animals, a scene often depicted on mosaic pavements, including several in Britain (Chedworth, Brading, Woodchester, Cirencester). He was on board the Argo.

562. **I could bring up my sons**: wholly egotistical, as indeed is most of Jason's speech from 545 onwards.

563. **have other sons**: already contradicting himself: see 558.

574. **Without the female sex**: marvellous words to a woman in love. He is not interested in her at all except as a mechanism for child-bearing.

577. **You are acting wrongly**: unusual for the chorus to take sides so decisively.

582. **In handsome words**: Euripides reflects a current controversy about the sophists. They claimed to train people to

32

make the worse cause appear the better. The borderline between making the weaker cause appear the stronger and making the morally wrong cause appear morally right was and is a blurred one.

585. **One word will throw you**: metaphor from wrestling, in Greek as in English. Medea claims that a wicked but eloquent man will be blind to some flaw in his own argument. In Jason's case it is that if he were really acting out of highmindedness, there was no reason why he should not have shared his plans with Medea.

585-7. Medea's coup de grace.

591. **Asiatic wife**: very bitter. A continuation of the Greek v. Barbarian theme.

597. **security**: Jason's primary concern, genuinely no doubt. Medea rejects it - but she does ensure her security with Aegeus before acting.

598. **prosperous future**: lit. 'blessed by the gods' (what gods? the protectors of oaths and marriages?) - bitterly sarcastic.

613. **Letters of introduction**: lit. 'tokens', a knucklebone cut in two so that the guest's half would fit the one retained by the host.

618. **A lying traitor's gifts carry no luck**: variant on a proverbial saying.

623. Medea displays jealousy.

626. **Will end with marriage lost**: ominous words.

627-62. *Second Stasimon.*

627. **Visitations of love**: the second formal song or *stasimon* from the chorus, again consisting of two pairs of matching stanzas without a rounding-off verse or *epode*. Euripides was charged with writing choral lyrics irrelevant to the action. Not here. The themes of this stasimon are two: love and exile.

632. **your golden bow**: Aphrodite is given the attributes of Eros. There seems to be a contrast between her inspiration of gentle love, and of violent passion (symbolized by the weapons).

635. **Innocence**: sophrosyne, the most untranslatable of Greek moral values, lit. something like 'saving wisdom', often rendered 'temperance' (which is misleading) or 'self-control' (which is inadequate). It has been called the characteristic ancient Greek virtue. On the contrary: they talked so much about it because they did not in general possess it.

640. **the dread Cyprian**: Aphrodite. The title is used in Homer (though only in *The Iliad* 5). She came to Greece via Cyprus,

where she was worshipped at Paphos, though the title may originally derive from a root meaning 'blooming'.

641. shrewdly: lit. 'sharp-minded'. The only occurrence of this particular Greek word - perhaps, therefore, coined by Euripides, who was well-known for his capacity for inventing words.

644. A stateless refugee: see on 255 (the same word appears in the Greek). The second half of the choral ode prepares our minds for the arrival of Aegeus.

663-823. *Third Episode: Aegeus and Medea.*

663. All happiness to you, Medea: Aegeus enters from the audience's left (from the country by convention). Some critics from Aristotle (*Poetics* 1451b20) onward have criticized the scene which follows as a lengthy diversion from the main plot, contrived to give Medea an escape-line. In fact the scene serves a variety of dramatic purposes. (a) It was probably, though not certainly, part of the tradition and therefore expected, perhaps also anticipated by the poet's own play *Aegeus,* though the date of this is not known. (b) It does provide the needed escape-route and a city for Medea to find a home in. (c) Aegeus, self-centred but courteous and firm, contrasts with the other king, Creon, weak, rude and blustering. (d) Above all, the childlessness of Aegeus gives Medea her plan for revenge. The scene is thus pivotal. Aegeus is to move from childlessness to fatherhood, Jason from fatherhood to childlessness. Nor should we forget a measure of political topicality in the contrast between Athens and Corinth: the two cities were drawn into hostility as Athens tried to expand her trade in the west at Corinth's expense, and in 435 Corcyra, a Corinthian colony, broke with Corinth, and in 433 allied with Athens. Corinth was Sparta's ally against Athens in the great war which was about to start.

Medea and Aegeus speak as old friends, but tradition does not seem to record a previous meeting. In Neophron's lost play (intr. sect. 6) Aegeus goes to Corinth in order to consult Medea about the oracle.

665-6. Aegeus, son of Pandion the wise!: this identifies the newcomer for the audience. Pandion himself was son of a Cecrops who was the eighth mythical king of Attica. Pandion's statue was visible on the Acropolis (Pausanias 1,5,3) and familiar enough to Athenians. There are other versions of Aegeus' birth. Aegeus was father of Theseus, the greatest of all Athenian heroes. Lasting childlessness for Aegeus would have spelled obscurity for Athens.

34

The Aegean Sea bears his name.

667. **oracle of Apollo**: and, before Apollo arrived, of Earth. Delphi was later famous for political consultations. But the great majority of individuals who consulted oracles came with domestic problems, usually about childlessness or crop-failure. In Euripides *Ion* the temple-attendant at Delphi sees Creusa approaching and asks 'Crops or children?' (303). This is interestingly parallel with traditional African society in twentieth-century Ghana where Margaret Field in *Search for Security* showed that the majority of oracle-consultations are on these two topics, with crops extending into other forms of business anxiety.

This line begins a long passage of *stichomythia* in the Greek (see on 324), obscured in translation.

668. **The centre of the earth**: lit. 'the navel', of which representations in stone may be seen in Delphi. According to legend, Zeus released two eagles to fly round the earth in different directions: they met at Delphi.

673. **I am married**: ancient commentators tell us that he married first Melite, and after her Chalciope; later, Aethra, the mother of Theseus.

675. **Too subtle**: oracular answers were often difficult or ambiguous to cover the oracle's reputation. Thus, in a famous, though apparently lucid, example, Croesus was told that if he crossed the river Halys he would destroy a great empire (Aristotle *Rhetoric* 1407a). He did - his own.

679-81. **'not to unstop the wineskin's neck'**: an ingenious paraphrase, since the Delphic oracles were normally in dactylic hexameters and Euripides was writing in iambic trimeters, so that he had to recast the traditional answer in a different rhythm. The mythical original is recorded in Plutarch's *Life of Theseus* (3):

> Great leader of the people, the wineskin's neck is not
>
> To be unstopped before you reach the common
>
> > folk of Athens.

and interpreted to mean that he should not have had sexual relations with a woman before reaching Athens.

682. **sailed to Corinth**: instead of taking the overland route he has gone down to the port of Itea, sailed to Corinth, with a view to

35

reaching Troezen by land, and sailing across the bay to Athens. Herodotus (4,179) says that Jason went from Iolcus to Delphi by boat round Greece rather than by land.

683. the King of Troezen, Pittheus, son of Pelops: Pelops was father of Atreus and grandfather of Agamemnon. Pittheus, another son, read the oracle, and in one form of the story, made Aegeus drunk, so that he fathered Theseus on the princess Aethra.

689. But you are looking: something in Medea's last words (as she perhaps intended) jerks Aegeus out of his own problems into an awareness of her needs.

698. Oh, passionately: sarcastic: two lines later she suggests the real objects of his passion.

709-10. I touch your beard as a suppliant, embrace your knees : both standard acts of supplication. For the second time Medea kneels to a man, in order to get her own way (see on 324).

717. put an end to your sterility: Medea's name might be taken as cognate with a word meaning 'sex-organ' (also *medos*). For a different word-play see on 402.

723. once you can get to Athens: this is so dramatically important that Aegeus repeats it three times in this speech. Asylum is granted her at Athens *provided she can effect her own escape*. We are kept in suspense over this till the last scene of all.

731. confirm your promise with an oath: the theme again, though Medea has little ground to trust the oaths of Greeks.

743. the taking of an oath safeguards me: Aegeus takes a simple prudential view.

746. Earth...Sun: see on 148. They appear together in an oath in Homer *The Iliad* 19,258-9 and in inscriptions.

759. Hermes, protector of travellers: Aegeus' departure is strangely precipitate, without a word to Medea. Hermes was the power of the cairn, and so of wild mountain ways. He protected the shepherds' flocks. He was naturally the protector of travellers, a traveller himself as the gods' messenger, and the guide of souls travelling to the underworld.

764. Justice, daughter of Zeus: one of the three Horai or Seasons, the others being Eunomia (lawfulness) and Peace, children of Zeus and Themis (see on 160).

770. Where I shall find safe mooring: we continue to be reminded of the voyage of Argo.

774. First I'll send a slave: stage-direction for the appearance of the nurse.

789. **I'll anoint**: there is a difficulty here. There is no obvious opportunity for her to do so. She would normally leave the stage for the next choral lyric (824-65), but she is addressed in the second half of this in language which means that she must be present. Most editors, and presumably this translator, treat it as an oversight, but it is a glaring one, and it is perhaps better to suppose that she is absent for the first part of the chorus, returning for the third stanza. Choral lyrics cover an indefinite period of dramatic time.

792. **I will kill my sons**: the first statement of her purpose.

795. **my darling children**: we are not to suppose that she does not care or that they are mere tools of her vengeance. She cares intensely, but the hatred for Jason to which her love has turned is deeper still. Jason cared for the children, and for her only as their breeder. She cared for Jason first, and the children as the consequence of that love.

797. **The laughter of my enemies I will not endure**: cf. 1049 below. This is Medea's form of pride.

799. **no refuge from despair**: lit. 'from evils'. But Aegeus offers the refuge from evils in the external sense, not from her inward struggles. Her revenge on the once-loved Jason means killing the still-loved children. The translation, though free, is justified.

804. **new bride**: this is the only appearance in the whole of surviving Greek literature of the word rendered 'new', lit. 'new-yoked'. See on 641.

809. **dangerous to my enemies**: Page quotes Lessing, 'Moral excellence in Greece consisted no less in unremitting hatred of your foes than in unalterable love towards your friends,' and cites passages from the poets Archilochus, Solon, Theognis and Pindar as well as the tragedians, contrasting the words of Socrates in Plato that one should never do wrong, even in requiting a wrong inflicted (*Crito* 49B).

813. **you must not do this!**: the chorus rebuke Medea as firmly as they have rebuked Jason (577).

817. **to deal Jason the deepest wound**: in killing not Jason but innocent children to hurt him, Medea becomes a moral monster. We now know Medea's motive for the infanticides.

824-65. *Third Stasimon.*

824. **The people of Athens, sons of Erechtheus**: the third of the

37

set choral lyrics, again two pairs of matching stanzas without an epode. For the argument that Medea must leave at this point, returning at the beginning of the third stanza, see on 789. The song is wholly relevant to the context, passing from a magnificent hymn in praise of Athens - cf. Sophocles' similar hymn to Athens in his Oedipus at Colonus 668ff. - (not the attitude of Corinthians at the time of the play) to Medea's criminal plan. An ancient commentator sums up their theme: 'It is the chorus' hope that the juxtaposition will turn her from the murder of her children: it is improbable that people of such pious wisdom will welcome a murderess.'

Erechtheus was the legendary primal Athenian, himself child of Earth (Herodotus 8,55); his temple stood and stands on the acropolis. There was some confusion between him and Erichthonius, divine son of Hephaestus and either Athene or Earth. The myth explains 'children of blessed gods' and 'grew from holy soil'. They claimed to be autochthonous, 'born of the land'.

826. **unscorched by invasion**: this was not true: there had been invasions (like that of the Persians in 480). It was certainly not to remain true. In the war which was on the horizon Pericles chose to withdraw the people within the walls of Athens, allow the Spartans to invade and scorch the land, and rely on their navy to import food. But it had not been seriously occupied. Thucydides (1,2,5), an Athenian himself, says that the reason was that the soil was so poor that is was not worth invading.

829. **glories of knowledge...pastured**: a clear metaphor and interesting claim. Pisistratus had developed Athens as a cultural and intellectual centre in the sixth century. In this regard its greatest glory was to come, in the fourth century, with Plato and Aristotle first, and then Epicurus and Zeno, the first of each pair a citizen, the second an immigrant.

831-2. **Harmony...the nine virgin Muses of Pieria**: the nine were given names and later (not at this period) specialized functions: Clio (history), Melpomene (tragedy), Thalia (comedy), Erato (love-lyric), Calliope (epic), Euterpe (lyric), Terpsichore (dance), Urania (astronomy), Polyhymnia (sacred song). They are not to be treated as artificial adjuncts tacked on to verses, but as real powers of inspiration. *Music* (much wider then than our word, and including literature and some science, but not the visual arts)

38

was the thing they inspired, and a *Museum* not a collection of dead objects, however edifying, but their temple and a centre of creative production and scholarship.

Pieria was a district of Macedonia whose name was transferred to the region of Mt. Helicon, their sacred mountain, not far from Delphi where Apollo, god of the arts, held court.

Harmony is difficult. It is not our musical harmony, which is *symphonia* (our symphony), a 'sounding together'. *Harmonia* means 'fitting properly', and here suggests that when all the Muses work together something new is produced. According to normal traditions she was daughter of Ares and Aphrodite, married to Cadmus of Thebes.

835-6. **Aphrodite...Cephisus**: Aphrodite is in myth the mother of Harmony. She was a goddess of fertility and flowers: by rivers all is green and flowery. Cephisus is one of the rivers of Athens, and in antiquity never dried up even in summer. The river-god was in myth one of the ancestors of the Athenians.

841. **roses**: sacred to Aphrodite. The word 'rose' comes from Persia; the flower reached Greece via Asia Minor and Syria, and may have come with the worship of the goddess; the first roses of spring were offered to her.

844. **Loves**: Eros is the god of love. As passion can multiply, so can the god of passion. On a relief in Athens we see a procession of Erotes as worshippers. But whereas Eros is a fearsome power who shatters lives, the Erotes become the tiresome little *putti* of Renaissance art.

845. **excellence in every art**: the Greek *arete* is best rendered 'excellence'. Later it comes to be used for ethical virtue, but at this stage means practical effectiveness in other spheres.

850. **pollution**: this related to a variety of actions in the wrong place (for example, sexual intercourse, birth or death in a sanctuary), and to some actions at any time, homicide and especially killing of a close relative, incest, cannibalism, whether or not the act was committed knowingly. For Oedipus see Sophocles *O.T.* 1415; *O.C.* 1132. Others might be tainted by touching a polluted person: this is why it is such a wonderful moment in Euripides *Heracles* (1398-1400) when Theseus takes the hand of the polluted Heracles. The normal cleansing ritual was through sacrifice but this might not always suffice (Hdt. 6,91). See R. Parker *Miasma* (Oxford 1983).

apparently and Medea actually in control.

869. **Jason**: she addresses him by name, as she did not in the earlier scene, in order to establish a superficial confidence. She must here kneel - for the third time - in supplication, to get her will.

881. **few enough**: but one, Aegeus, is sufficient.

884. **wise**: see on 635 'Innocence': the same root-word: the idea is of a deliberate prudence. Note the irony of Medea's words, and her self-control in being able to say what she does (886-8).

894. **Children, children!**: a stage-direction for their entry. Page points out the dramatic power of their frequent entries and exits: we think that each will be the last.

899. **There, children; take his hand**: this is dramatically of great power. It recalls 21, 496 and Jason's treachery. This leads her to think of her revenge and the death of the children: hence the tears.

900. **What pain the future hides from us**: an ancient commentator notes that Medea is speaking of the children's fate, but Jason understands the general human condition - a good example of dramatic irony. See 925.

902. **stretch out your hands**: yes they will. Their lives will be cut short as they stretch out their hands to her for mercy.

908. **I am pleased, Medea**: in the Greek 'wife', which is more powerful. Jason is complacent.

925. **thinking about these children**: again dramatic irony. The words have a different meaning for speaker and hearer.

928. **tears come naturally to us**: Shakespeare *King John* 3,1,14 'A woman naturally born to tears'.

930. **I'm their mother**: strictly 'I went through the process of bearing them', echoing 250.

945. **She will, if she's like other women**: grimly ironic and ambiguous from Medea, who is *not* like other women (see on 1339) but who knows how to get her way with males. But the words are perhaps better given to Jason. The earliest MSS did not give speakers' names.

949. **The dress and golden coronet**: the gifts that were mentioned in 786 above.

954. All references to the Sun are significant in this play.

974. **longs for**: the same word as passionate love: Medea's

40

passionate longing for Jason is now a passionate longing to hurt him. This (and the next line) contains a grim dramatic irony.

976-1001. *Fourth Stasimon.*

976. **Now I have no more hope**: the fourth *stasimon* or formal choral dance and song, again in two pairs of matching stanzas without a final **epode**, and again directly and totally relevant. But there is a difference. In the first three the opening stanzas have been general, the last two have focussed on the immediate action. Here, as the death of the children becomes imminent, the whole song is immediate.

985. **Preparing her bridal beauty**: one word in the Greek, and a very rare one, found only twice elsewhere, centuries later. The whole phrase is very striking.

1002-1250. *Fifth Episode: Medea and Tutor, and Medea and Messenger.*

1005. **Isn't that good news?**: there is no better example of the dramatic irony which permeates the play. The last hope was that the princess would reject the gifts. The tutor's good news spells disaster.

1015. **will bring you home**: i.e. from exile. The Greek means 'bring back' or 'bring down'.

1016. **send home**: i.e. to death: she takes the meaning 'bring down' (i.e. to Hades). Irony again.

1020. **as on other days**: but to no purpose.

1021. **O children, children!**: compare 894. The fluctuations in Medea's mind in this magnificent speech are marvellously conveyed. So are the extraordinary ambiguities with which she speaks of their destiny.

1027. **hold the torches high**: a feature of the marriage ceremony.

1034. **wrap my dead body**: in modern Africa, as in ancient Greece, one of the curses of childlessness is that there in no-one to care for the burial. To be unburied, without the proper rites, was in Greek thought to be deprived of the passage to the relative peace of the underworld. Hence the political furore at the failure of the commanders to gather up the dead and rescue the survivors after the naval battle of Arginusae in 406. The theme of non-burial dominates Sophocles *Antigone*.

1049. **To laugh at me**: see on 797.

1054. **sacrifice**: a marvellous touch. Compare Othello in Shakespeare's play (5,2,63): 'O perjur'd woman, thou dost stone my heart,/And mak'st me call what I intend to do/A murther, which I thought a sacrifice.'

1059. **fiends of hate**: personified powers of Vengeance: see also 1260.

1064. **The thing's done now**: her purpose may fluctuate, but the action she has already taken is inexorable.

1073. **there, not here!**: 'there' is the usual Greek euphemism for the afterworld when contrasted with 'here' meaning life on earth.

1078-80. **I understand...my resolve**: Medea's personality is complex, and her mind deeply divided. The ingenious Roman poet Ovid makes his Medea say (in another context) 'Desire persuades me one way, Reason another. I see and approve the better course; I follow the worse.' *(Met.* 7,19-21).

1081-1115. *Choral Interlude.*

1081. **I have often engaged in arguments**: this is not a formal choral lyric. It is in anapaests (see on 96), quickened from speech-rhythms. The almost prosaic touch serves to reduce the tension. It is. a remarkable passage, put in the mouth of women from Corinth, questioning whether children are worth it, challenging the accepted social values.

1084. **Than is suitable for women**: Athenian males, with their very 'Victorian' attitude to women, would unsuspectingly approve this.

1085. **too have intelligence**: not quite what the chorus say. They speak of the Muse (see on 831-2), claiming inspiration (rather than intelligence) leading to wisdom. The Greeks had prophetesses and males have usually admitted female 'intuition'.

1116-1250. *Medea and Messenger.*

1116. **Friends, I have long been waiting**: it is not clear whether Medea goes off-stage during this meditation, or, as the translation implies, remains in view. We are waiting in suspense for the murder of the children: it still has not happened. Medea is looking out to the audience's right, to the city and palace (see on 446, 663). She is waiting for news from the palace. It was a stock aspect of Greek tragedy that, although drama is action not narration, the climactic scene should take place off-stage and be narrated by a messenger; it might be too gory or too awesome to take place in view of the audience, or even impossible to stage. Often, as here, the messenger blurts out his essential news in a line or two and then elaborates it in a highly rhetorical speech.

42

1120. **fearful news**: lit. 'evil'. Medea knows that it is a crime; but it is evil because it spells the children's death.

1126. **her father Creon**: this is unexpected.

1127. **Your news is excellent**: another paradox: the bad news is good. See on 1005 where the good news was bad.

1144. **Our mistress**: Glauce is brilliantly characterized. Greek women married young; she will be barely in her teens. We see her admiration for Jason (no doubt he had been spinning tales of his adventures), her pouting dislike of the reminder of the other woman, her fit of teenage temper, her delight in the splendid clothes, her eagerness to try them on, her smiling at her reflection, and her parade to let the dress hang out.

1149. **upset**: the Greek is a technical medical term, odd on a servant's lips.

Your husband: even Jason's man so addresses her.

1161. **a bright mirror**: not of course of glass, but of polished silver or bronze.

1162. **lifeless**: a tremendous stroke of irony.

1172. **Pan**: originally perhaps a shepherds' god, with the same root as *pasture,* then an awesome power of the wildwood who might cause pan-ic. An ancient commentator writes 'People of old used to think that those who suddenly fell over had been struck in their minds, generally by Pan or Hecate.' It was felt that a god's appearance or handiwork should be immediately acknowledged with a 'cheerful cry'. Equally, when the old servant realized that such a cry was inappropriate, she needed to correct her mistake: so she followed it with a shriek *(kokytos).* See Page.

1181-2. **while a fast runner**: the exact meaning of these two lines is elusive in the original, but the point is the speed of her recovery of consciousness.

1187. **a stream of...fire**: a vivid visual picture preparing us for the horrid visual details to follow.

1200. **like gum-drops from a pine-tree's bark**: a powerful simile.

1210. **let me die with you**: irony again. It is an immediate response to extreme grief, but not a prayer he would be likely to wish or expect to have such immediate fulfilment.

1213. **As ivy**: a familiar metaphor, but again ironical, for it is often used of a bride clinging to bridegroom for life, not of father to daughter for death.

1221. **such a sight as tears were made for**: a difficult phrase in the original: this is as reasonable a rendering as any.

1224. **As for human life**: Euripides' messengers often end with a philosophical reflection on life generalized from the scene they have reported.

a shadow: so the lyric poet Pindar earlier in the century wrote 'man is a dream of a shadow' (*Pythians* 8,95).

1230. **Prosperity increases; happiness never**: the distinction is of great importance, both in philosophy and life. Prosperity depends on fortune and consists in externals, riches, good health and the like. Happiness is an inward state; there was some discussion as to whether prosperity was a necessary concomitant of full happiness, but no doubt that the two are not identical. See for example the treatment in Aristotle *Nicomachean Ethics* 1,8,1098b9ff.

1232. **on Jason**: strange that the chorus of Corinthian women should see the death of their king and princess as a calamity *for Jason*.

1245. **frontier of despair**: the translator has changed the metaphor. The Greek word signifies the post which formed both the start and finish of a race. A potent ambiguity: the end of the misery of life with Jason is the beginning of misery of life without the children she will murder.

1250. **Life has been cruel to me**: in the view of many scholars (but see on 789, 824, 1116) this is the first time Medea has left the stage since her original entry at 214. If they are right it is certainly a powerful effect, placing the spotlight (as it were) on the children's death.

1251-1292. *Fifth Stasimon: death of the children within.*

1251. **Earth, awake!**: the chorus sing a two-stanza song with dance-movement as the tension builds up. The invocation of Earth and Sun is important. See on 148. We must remember that, as she has more than once reminded us (406, 746, 954), the Sun is Medea's grandfather.

1252. **Look! Look down**: in the original 'Look-down, look', an effect Euripides liked, moving from the compound verb to the simple.

1260. **fiend of vengeance**: she is described as an Erinys or Fury, driven by an Alastor, the personification of Vengeance ('fiend of hate' at 1059). In Aeschylus' trilogy *The Oresteia* the Furies seeking vengeance for Orestes' murder of his mother Clytemnestra, having invisibly driven him from the stage at the end of the second

44

play, appear in terrifying form in *The Eumenides.*

1263. Symplegades: the Clashing Rocks. See on 2, 433; intr. sect. 7.

1264. the barbarous sea: lit. 'hostile to strangers'. The Black Sea. The Greeks in the hope of allaying the hostility called it Euxine, 'friendly to strangers', a name it still bears, as they called the dreaded Furies the Eumenides, 'kindly ones'. Note how deep in the Greek way of life was the thought that behind the forces of nature which affect us externally and the emotions which affect us within are superhuman powers.

1270. the guilty house: the house is a vital concept for the understanding of Greek society, and one we have largely, though not entirely, lost. It is, in the broadest sense, the family, but extended not nuclear, and with a sense of solidarity in power or guilt. In Corinth the Bacchiadae married within the family. At Athens when murder was laid at the door of the Alcmaeonidae, 700 households were banished (Hdt. 9,72).

At this point, a child's scream rings out: the Greek text of course gives us not a stage direction but the sound of a scream, outside the pattern of the verses. The chorus sing their response, again in two stanzas. But in the first the voices of the children in the metre of ordinary dialogue twice break through their song, and in the second, the children's voices having died away into an ominous silence they themselves break up their song with two corresponding couplets of spoken words. Gory action usually takes place off-stage. See on 1116, and note Horace's advice 'Medea should not slaughter the children in view of the people'. *(Ars Poetica* 185).

1275. Shall we go in?: by convention the chorus do not intervene, though they sometimes come close to doing so.

1282. There was but one: it is over. The chorus sing a sad little song about a mother who killed her children. One of the characteristics of Greek tragedy is to take the human drama (itself of course usually mythical in origin but human as it confronts us) and take it up into the poetry of myth in this way so that we see it as reflecting issues and values which are with us always. In the most familiar version of the story Ino, daughter of Cadmus and Harmonia, was married to Athamas, king of Orchomenus, by whom she had two sons, Learchus and Melicertes. Her sister Semele bore Dionysus to Zeus, but perished through seeing Zeus in his glory. Ino brought up her nephew, and in so doing incurred

45

Hera's anger, who drove her and Athamas mad. Athamas killed Learchus, and Ino jumped into the sea with Melicertes in her arms. They were divinized, she under the name of Leucothea ('the white goddess'), he as Palaemon ('the wrestler', associated with the Isthmian Games). This song however is evidence that the most familiar version of the story (which has many variants) to the Athenians of 431 B.C. was one in which Ino first killed both children and then jumped into the sea. Euripides wrote a play on Ino; we know the plot but not the date (before 425).

1293-1414. *Exodos: Jason and Medea (3)*.

1297. **soar on wings to the sky's abyss**: we are still in tension about her escape: see on 723. This, which Jason voices as an impossibility, is an anticipation of what is to happen - a further example of dramatic irony.

1304. **before Creon's family murder them**: in a story known at second hand from a certain Creophylus, Medea killed Creon for an unstated reason, and escaped to Athens, leaving the children, who were too young for her to take, in sanctuary in the temple of Hera. Creon's relatives disregarded the sanctuary and killed them, spreading the rumour that Medea had killed them before leaving. (In another version Medea is queen of Corinth, and the women of Corinth, not liking being subject to a foreign witch, rise against her and kill her children.) Euripides has turned the rumour into his substantive plot, and in these lines alludes to the more familiar story. We are told that the Athenians regarded the play as unpatriotic because Euripides transferred the guilt of the murders away from the Corinthians, their political enemies, and even spread a rumour that he was bribed to do so (intr. sects. 6-7). The situation is again charged with irony.

1308. **to kill me too**: the perfect egoist.

1317. **Jason!**: the third and final confrontation which leaves Medea triumphant and Jason broken. The visual dramatic effect must have been spectacular. The theatre (intr. sect. 2) was equipped with a crane (Gk. *mechane,* Lat. *machina*) by which a carriage, decked to appear as a dragon-drawn chariot, with Medea and the dead children in it, was swung high over the stage. (There are some who think that the appearance was staged differently, but this is the most probable account.)

1321. **the Sun**: the secret of her escape is out, an airborne car provided by her grandfather, the Sun. The chorus has called on the

46

Sun (1252), Jason will appeal to the Sun (1327), but the Sun aids and abets her action.

1322. **to save us**: a noun in the Greek, the same that Jason has used at 597 of children as a source of security.

1327. **outface both Sun and Earth**: it was a standard Greek idea that a polluted person was an offence to the Sun; so with Oedipus when it comes out that he has killed his father, married his mother and is under his own curse (Sophocles *O.T.* 1425); he is polluted even though his offence was not deliberate. Jason cannot accommodate himself to the idea of a Sun-god who supports Medea in her actions. See on 850.

1330. **a land of savages**: see on 536.

1335. **The vengeance due for your sins**: no doubt this is what Jason means, but it is not what he says. He says 'Your vengeance', ambiguous between 'the vengeance due to you' and 'the vengeance due from you'.

my lovely Argo's hull: here more than anywhere we get the sense that Jason is living in the past. He has this one achievement behind him, and he is (so to speak) resting on his oars.

1339. **In all Hellas**: precisely, because no Greek woman loved with such open passion, because Athenian women in particular were trained to be obedient to their husbands. So Pericles in Thucydides 2,45 'That woman's is the glory who is least talked about by man for good or bad.' But were there some Athenian males in the audience who suddenly wondered with a twinge of anxiety what might be going on underneath their wife's façade and what would happen if the mask of decorum were removed?

1342. **a tiger; a Tuscan Scylla**: strictly a lioness (137-8). Scylla was a nymph turned into a sea-monster by Circe, with twelve feet and six heads each with three rows of teeth, and baying dogs round her waist. She menaced one side of the Straits of Messina, opposite the whirlpool Charybdis, as Odysseus found to his cost. The sea to the west of the Straits was called the Tuscan or Etruscan Sea.

1346. **polluted fiend**: lit. 'doer of shame'. The ancient commentator says that this line was hissed by the audience. There is a curious anecdote preserved from 150 years later (Athenaeus 13,582C quoting Macho). Lais, the well-known courtesan, met Euripides in a park and asked him what he meant by writing this line. He was taken aback by her effrontery, and said 'Aren't you a doer-of-shame?' She replied with another line from his lost play *Aeolus* 'What is shameful, if it does not seem so to those who practise it?' On the face of it, there is nothing objectionable in the *Medea* line, but the anecdote suggests that the 'doer-of-shame' was a word with strong obscene connotations.

1348-9. I have lost...I begot: the words are self-centred, the bride and children treated simply as instruments of his happiness, but it is unlikely that the males in the audience will have found anything odd or abnormal about them: they represent the accepted social values.

1355. laugh at me: she is obsessive about this. See 797, 1049, and, below, 1361.

1360. and that is right: almost 'necessary', the necessary outcome of his betrayal, and the appropriate requital for his heartlessness to her.

1361. You suffer too: the beginning of a short passage of *stichomythia*, line-for-line exchange in the Greek. See on 324.

1362. It is true: this is vital. Medea is suffering too.

1365. my hand: but this is the hand with which he pressed hers, the hand with which he made promises and professions. See 21, 496, 899.

1369. modest: the concept rendered 'Innocence' at 635 and 'wise' at 884. See on 635. Again we wonder: Athenian males did not always preserve *sophrosyne*. What if their wives broke out?

the whole world lost: i.e. 'the injury is to you the whole world lost'.

1373. Yes - they know the vileness of your heart: Jason is getting the worst of the argument and knows it. Medea has made a genuine point; he can only cap it with cheap abuse.

1379. Hera Acraea: this conforms to the tradition: see on 1304. Acraea means 'in the height'; it is also a title of Aphrodite. Hera Acraea is known only in connection with Medea and the children, which leads some to think that Medea was originally close to or identified with Hera, and that human sacrifice was part of the cult.

1382. an annual feast and sacrifice: Euripides was fascinated by the relation of myth and ritual, and loved to link his dramas of a past age with the ritual of his own times. This is, for example, strong at the end of *Iphigeneia among the Taurians*. She knows the impiety of her own act, for which atonement must be made. But there may be a reminiscence of the other version where the

48

Corinthians committed the murder.

1383. **this impious murder**: she is under no illusions about the ambiguities of her action - a just vengeance and an impious crime at once.

1384. **city of Erechtheus**: see on 824.

1385. **Aegeus, son of Pandion**: see on 665-6.

1387. **a timber from the Argo's hull**: the most unkindest cut of all. Jason's great exploit will bring his death. An ancient commentator tells us the story. Jason dedicated the stern in Hera's temple. He was visiting the temple when it fell and killed him. In another version he was sleeping in the shadow of the old ship, the shade of his glory, when a rotting timber fell on him, his heroism in ruins. Neophron (intr. sect. 6) introduced a variant whereby Jason died by hanging. Medea at this point has the gift of prophecy.

1389. **The curse**: lit. 'Fury', a role in which Medea has appeared (1260).

1390. **Justice**: see on 764.

1391. **What god**: she is turning his words (1327) back on him. For the soil of Athens and the Sun conspire to save her.

1392. **guest-deceiver**: The Greek word *xenos* is ambiguous between guest and host, stranger and friend. Medea was stranger and friend, his host in Colchis and his guest in Greece.

1396. **You grieve too soon**: compare 1033 above on the question of childless old age.

1405. **Zeus**: he finally calls on the highest of the gods. See on 148.

1407. **savage beast**: lit. 'lioness': see on 1342.

1413. **Would God I had not bred them**: a line that echoes the nurse's vain wish at the very beginning of the play (line 1).

1415. **Many are the Fates**: a stock Euripidean ending, found also in *Alcestis, Andromache, Bacchae* (with a small variant) and *Helen.* It may have been written for *Alcestis,* which it fits. Why did he repeat it? Some scholars have seen it as a kind of signature, others as a way of scorning the myths. But it is oddly inapposite here, and it seems more likely that actors took it from *Alcestis* and added it where they fancied. G.M.A. Grube wrote: 'The familiar tag which the chorus sings it walks off the stage (it is found at the end of three other plays) brings no comfort. The play ends in violent discord; there is no peace here, only Violence and Hate.'

ELECTRA

Note: the numbers refer to lines in the Greek text. They appear at the top of each page of the Penguin translation, but do not correspond line by line.

1-166. Prologue. *The peasant, to whom Electra has been married off, sets the scene. Electra joins him. They go off, and Orestes and Pylades enter. Electra returns and sings an exquisite solo (112-66).*

1. As in *Medea* Euripides begins not with a noble but with a peasant, though before the play is over we find that he has been the only truly gentle person. Here the audience must have been puzzled already, as the stage building will have had some indication - thatch round the door or something such - that it represents not a palace or temple but a cottage. The first play of the day began early, so a scene in the early dawn was not implausible. He outlines the mythical background to the play (intr. sect. 12).

Argos: almost a pun, since without the capital it means 'plain' in Greek.

Inachus: the local river, as often personified as a semi-divine being.

5. **Dardanus:** ancestor of the Trojans, grandfather of Tros, and great-grandfather of Ilus (eponymous heroes of Troy and Ilium).

6-7. **on our temple walls:** normal Greek practice: religious and political life were intertwined.

10. **Thyestes:** see intr. sect. 12.

11. **Tantalus:** see intr. sect. 12.

18. **Phocis:** fertile agricultural region of central Greece, of which Strophius was the legendary king.

22. **a prince:** an interesting example of the editing of Greek texts. The MSS have 'an Argive'. But the peasant is an Argive: so this must be wrong. It was the great nineteenth-century scholar Porson who proposed a word, similar enough to have been easily miscopied, meaning 'prince'.

33. **To anyone who killed Orestes:** this seems to be Euripides'

invention. Dramatically it may suggest that Aegisthus makes a concesssion to the daughter at the cost of the son.

34. **wife to me**: this startling innovation on the traditional legend must have caused a stir among the audience.

35. **Mycenaeans**: Argos, with a fine fortress and early history of its own, lies close to the coast. Mycenae, the centre of power in the second millennium B.C., lies further inland: here Heinrich Schliemann excavated, found a gold mask, and thought (erroneously) that he had looked on Agamemnon's face. The peasant means that he belonged to the ancient nobility fallen into poverty. Argos, unlike Mycenae, carried contemporary political overtones, a city-state of the Peloponnese, tending to be anti-Spartan.

37-8. **when you're poor...**: Euripides was not afraid to challenge the attitudes of those in power.

43. **Aphrodite**: goddess of sexual passion.

50-3. **If any man thinks me a fool...**: like the Tutor in *Medea*, and many people in real life, the peasant becomes sententious and didactic.

54. **O black night**: Electra enters with a pitcher on her head. She is poorly dressed and her hair is cropped short. There is no indication in the original of the peasant going out and returning, and this is unlikely. But Electra thinks she is alone; so he must step to one side and watch. Remember that there is nothing to identify her: she gradually reveals who she is. There are no stage-directions in the original.

nurse the golden stars: this simple phrase has caused a great deal of trouble. We do not need to worry about a myth in which Night was mother of the Stars, or an erudite suggestion that night helps the stars to grow because her darkness increases their brightness. Rather, night enfolds the stars in her embrace. But the image suggests her yearning for the baby she has not had.

58. **the insolence of Aegisthus**: this is *hybris,* arrogance to be visited with Nemesis (hence 'show the gods'), but also violation. Electra, who is sexually unbalanced (her name means 'Unwed') feels that she has been raped by Aegisthus - an interesting and important psychological point in view of her mother's relation with him. Note her expressed motive for her humble service.

59. **to my father's spirit**: in one pattern of Greek belief the body returned to earth, the *psyche* or soul to the upper air.

60. **Tyndareos' daughter**: she does not name her mother, nor offer credence to the tale that Zeus was her grandfather (approaching Leda in swan's form). Tyndareos or Tyndareus was king of Sparta and husband to Leda.

62. **other sons**: she is jealous of her mother. Sophocles also mentions children of the marriage. From other sources we know of a daughter named Erigone (herself a tragic theme) and a son called Aletes.

71. **Should do my share**: not the motive she has just privately admitted (see on 58). But we should not charge her with insincerity, only with inconsistency and fluctuating moods.

76. **He likes to find the house...**: male Athenians will have applauded, but Electra is play-acting and there is a shock coming to them.

77. **Go, then, if you wish**: 'The way he humours her is a delightful touch. After all, it won't hurt her!' - J. D. Denniston.

80-1. **Pious words...**: the rustic philosopher again! The words are a little more biting than they seem at first.

82. **Pylades**: a curiously awkward exit and entry. By convention the country lay to the audience's left, the city to the audience's right. They must therefore come in from the left, so the others must go out right; they are not going far. Pylades was son of Strophius, king of Phocis, and his wife Anaxibia, Agamemnon's sister. The name of Pylades identifies the speaker as probably Orestes, but in the Greek Orestes identifies himself by name.

83. **shared your home**: friendship between host and guest was a sacred tie.

87. **Apollo's oracle**: at Delphi. This is an emendation: the Greek has 'mysteries'.

92. **killed a lamb**: to the gods of Olympus offerings were of white animals on a high altar with the fatal blow leaving the wound open to the sky; to the dead, of black animals, with the throat cut from underneath so that the blood fell into a trench and went down into the earth. The assumption here is that the dead, as in Homer, survive in Hades under the earth (contrast on 59), and require blood (or its surrogate, red wine) to give them strength.

96. **near the border**; he is playing it safe: note how he takes cover at Electra's entrance.

107. **a slave-girl**: a stage-direction for Electra's re-entry. Note that he does not recognize her in her poor clothes, cropped hair (in

mourning, not, as he thinks, as a slave) and at her menial task. Note too that entries and exits took some time: here five lines.

112. **Quicken your step**: Electra sings and dances a great solo or monody. It consists of two pairs of stanzas, each pair consisting of *strophe* and matching *antistrophe*, a dance 'wound' one way and 'unwound' the other, probably in the orchestra (intr. sect. 2). The first pair, with the pot on her head, must have been spectacular. There are however two interruptions in between the stanzas (125-6, 150-6), perhaps chanted without dance-movement. The words are addressed to herself, 'naively' says an ancient commentator.

123-4. **Killed by your wife and her lover**: in Aeschylus Clytemnestra commits the murder, in Sophocles and Euripides both lovers.

140. **Take this jar**: addressed to a slave, which even a poor peasant would possess. The presence of another person (even a 'non-person' like a slave) would mar the effect of the self-communing, and Orestes has mentioned one person only. So we must suppose that this is a stage-direction for the entry of a 'dumb mask' or walking-on part, cf. the children in *Medea*. The second dance is performed without the pot on the head.

147. **nail tears cheek**: a common sign of grief, curiously rare in Homer, but frequent enough in Athens to be banned by Solon in the sixth century (Plutarch *Solon* 21). Beating the head is often associated with it. To cut the hair in mourning is found in many parts of the world, from Peru to India. It is an offering of a part of oneself, a sacrifice of growth, symbolically of life. Remember that the death took place many years before. Euripides intends our attitude to Electra to be ambivalent. We sympathize, but we are aware of a pathological obsession.

151. **As a swan**: bird metaphors are frequent in Greek poetry. In Aeschylus Electra and Orestes are compared to eagles *(Choephoroe* 247); in Sophocles Electra's lament is that of a nightingale *(Electra* 107). The swan is a fresh image, but the swan was (without justification) a symbol of filial piety (Eur. *Bacchae* 1365; Cicero *De Finibus* 2,33). There is no other reference to the snaring of the swans, though other birds were snared.

160. **the axe's edge**: but at 164 a two-edged sword. Both are in the tradition. In Homer the murder-weapon was a sword, in Stesichorus an axe, in Aeschylus a sword (though Clytemnestra calls for an axe to defend herself against Orestes), in Sophocles an

axe, elsewhere in this play an axe.

167-212. *Parodos. Arrival of chorus of unmarried girls, who invite Electra to join in their coming festival.*

167. Electra, daughter of Agamemnon: the chorus of local women join Electra in dance and song, addressing her by the title most precious to her. There are two matching stanzas (167-89, 190-212), each shared between chorus and soloist. This was a famous song, and we are told that at the end of the Peloponnesian War when Athens was totally defeated by the Spartan Lysander, she was saved from annihilation because a man from Phocis sang this song (Plutarch *Lysander* 15).

169. bred on mountain milk: instead of wine.

172. a festival: the Heraea or Hecatombaea (because a hecatomb or sacrifice of a hundred victims was offered). Hera's priestess drove from city to temple in a car drawn by cows, and evidently accompanied by unmarried girls. The festival involved some kind of reenactment of the sacred marriage between Hera and Zeus (symbolic of earth and sky) to ensure the fertility of the land; it included competitions in music and athletics.

174. Hera's temple: the great Heraeum, between Argos and Mycenae in a magnificent situation on a terraced site on a hill commanding the plain. The buildings have gone, but it remains impressive even in its desolation.

185. My dress in tatters: this is Electra's own choice, a necessity of her inner not her outer state. Euripides notoriously liked to bring on characters in rags - and with their souls in rags too.

190. Hera is great: a typical religious cry, almost a mantra, or prescribed sacred formula.

191. Borrow from me: then, as now, clothes for special occasions might be borrowed or hired.

194. honouring the gods; trying to appeal to her reason: useless.

211-2. my mother lies: her sexual obsessions burst out again.

213-431. *First Episode. Orestes and Pylades appear but do not reveal who they are. After a long dialogue between Orestes and Electra, the Peasant appears and welcomes the guests.*

213-4. Your mother's sister Helen: the chorus-leader breaks into the ordinary language and rhythms of conversation. Clytemnestra and Helen were sisters. Helen's abduction by Paris was the occasion of the Trojan War. There is a thought-link with Electra's song. Helen and Clytemnestra married the brothers Menelaus and

54

Agamemnon, and each abandoned her husband for another, Paris and Aegisthus.

215. **Look, friends**: she actually says 'I have snapped out of my dirges'.

216. **I see two men there**: this acts as a stage-direction for the emergence of Orestes and Pylades.

220. **Don't run away!**: this begins no fewer than 70 lines of *stichomythia*, line-for-line dialogue, broken only by two cries from Orestes.

221. **Phoebus Apollo!**: this serves also as a kind of stage-direction. There is a statue of Apollo near the door as protector of the house.

224. **There's no one living**: he comes near to revealing himself.

239. **My face is withered**: Electra's self-pity.

241. **my Scythian scalp**: the Scythians scalped their enemies (Herodotus 4,64). For the cutting of the hair in grief see on 147.

245. **He loves me from a distance**: spoken bitterly. It was a proverbial saying. Athenaeus (5,197D) quotes a 'very cynical aphorism' from an unknown tragedian, 'Friends living at a distance are no friends.'

246. **Tell me, Electra**: in the Greek he does not name her.

247. **a living death**: Electra making the worst of her state.

248. **I grieve for Orestes**: he thinks of his own disgrace and hers.

253. **generous-hearted**: she compensates, but reveals her instability. The overtones of class-consciousness are fascinating. Like the English 'gentleman' or 'noble', such words originally represented high birth and consequent social and political power. But the aristocracy might lose wealth and power, and a new middle-class achieve them. Moral values came into question. Some assumed and others challenged the view that only the highborn could be 'gentle' or 'noble'.

256. **For religious reasons?**: sexual abstinence in many cultures may be a permanent vow (as with Orphics, Orthodox monks, Catholic priests) or a temporary obligation (African warriors during military campaigns).

258. **He's pleased enough**: Orestes is a cynical aristocrat.

260. **he fears Orestes**: and self-satisfied.

262. **He seems**: preceded in the Greek by an astonished exclamation outside the verse-scheme.

263. **if the exile ever returns**: again bitter, cf. 245. She does not

55

name him in all these 70 lines of dialogue.

265. **for their lovers**: a bitter expression of her obsession.

275. **You insult him**: not without justification. He is already showing his weakness, and relying on her determination.

281. **When I have shed**: she sees herself as the actual killer.

282. **I wish**: the English stage-direction represents another gasping exclamation outside the metrical scheme: see on 230, 262.

283. **I should not recognize him**: irony.

285. **only one**: preparing for the recognition-scene.

289. **His body lies**: typical exaggeration from Electra, as we soon learn that he is buried in a tomb. In Homer his body was thrown out to the carrion birds and animals; in Aeschylus it received unceremonious burial. To be left unburied was indeed 'unspeakable', for it left the passage to the underworld unsecured. This is the theme of Sophocles *Antigone,* and *Ajax* too.

294-6. **For sympathy...**: the audience liked such sententious remarks, in character here with Orestes' oblique approach.

. 304. **stabled**: a word elsewhere used only of animals.

307. **sit at the loom**: normally slave's work, except for ceremonial work.

310. **never a feast**: we have just seen her refuse an invitation to one (175).

311. **myself a virgin**: this is not public knowledge: she is referring to her own embarrassment.

312. **Castor**: this is a puzzle. He and his brother Polydeuces or Pollux are normally brothers of Clytemnestra and Helen, and therefore Electra's uncles. There is no other reference to his courting of Electra: it seems to be Euripides' invention, and it is not easy to see the point of it. Castor, one of the 'heavenly twins', was translated to Olympus and the gods with his brother - and to the sky as the constellation Gemini. The son of a god might become a god if he served humankind well.

327. **Royal Aegisthus**: bitterly sarcastic.

331. **is not here**: Aegisthus' taunt is the same, to the very words, as Electra's (245).

337. **can't he kill one man?**: of course Agamemnon did not really master the Trojans single-handed; this is part of Electra's exaggerated idealization of him. And the real issue is the death of Clytemnestra. But Electra is reserving this to herself (281). Only, Aegisthus stands in the way.

339. **I see your husband**: equivalent to the stage direction.

344. **It's not right**: the established Athenian attitude.

345. **Dear husband**: she did not so address him earlier.

348. **Friends, forgive**: she is ashamed of his bluntness, and behaves like a princess, not a wife.

357. **You ought to have asked them in**: he rebukes her, and shows his hospitable nature.

360. **Men**: apparently attendants on Orestes and Pylades (one of whom returns as the Messenger: see 766), though the peasant no doubt has a small household of slaves: see on 140.

365. **to save Orestes' honour**: cf. 248.

366. **'poor Electra's husband'**: for her he does not exist in his own right.

367. **There's no clear sign**; the beginning of a highly sententious speech: see on 253. It reflects a current debate. But the sentiments come slightly oddly from Orestes; is he a wholly worthy son of the heroic Agamemnon?

369. **noble father...worthless son**: irony.

375-6 **poverty is a disease**: as Bernard Shaw argued centuries later.

384-5. **By the company they keep**: as in the proverb, voiced by Menander, 'Bad company corrupts good character', and quoted in the New Testament (1 *Cor.* 15,33).

392. **Whose messenger I am**: lit. 'for whose sake I have come' - even stronger dramatic irony.

399-400. **Human prognostications...Apollo's prophecies**: the contrast between divine infallibility and the fallibility of human prophets and priests was a current cliché. But it is fascinating here, since Euripides here and in a number of plays seems highly critical of the Delphic Oracle (cf. 1245), perhaps treating it as nothing but human manipulation.

404. **You fool**: the princess, not the wife, in marked contrast to 345. She thinks more of 'face' than of hospitality. By contrast in a folk-tale recorded in Ovid's *Metamorphoses* the worthy peasants Philemon and Baucis entertained gods unaware.

406. **Why not?**: a good down-to-earth answer, followed by a comment on real nobility of character.

410. **Tanaos**: or Tanos, a mountain-torrent, later the Luku, near the border of Arcadia as well as Sparta.

420. **Well, if you think it best**: the peasant is excellently

57

characterized. 'She'll rustle up something...I'd like to have a bit of money for once...But your belly doesn't contain any more because you're rich.'

432-486. *First Stasimon or choral song.*

432. **Famous were the ships**: this begins a formal song and dance from the chorus. It consists of two pairs of matching stanzas (432-41 = 442-51; 452-63 = 464-75), each consisting of a *strophe* ('winding') and matching *antistrophe* ('unwinding'), presumably a dance movement which is then reversed. The song ends with an *epode*, or final stanza (476-86), sung facing the audience. Choral songs are often used to place the events of the play in a wider background of myth. Euripides was charged with writing irrelevant choruses. Here the avenging of the murder of the Greek commander at Troy is relevantly placed in the context of the Trojan War. The song has four key themes: Achilles the athlete; light and fire, bright but destructive; Trojan War from glory to disaster (this is in its way an anti-war play); the Gorgon.

. 434. **dancing of oars**: a delightful metaphor linked with the religious personification of the waves as dancing nymphs.

438. **Thetis**: a sea-nymph, loved by the god Zeus and the human Peleus. She was destined to bear a son greater than his father: on learning this Zeus sensibly renounced her. The son was the hero Achilles.

439. **light-footed leaper**: Homer describes him as 'swift of foot'.

441. **the Simois river**: mountain stream, running down from a spur of Mt. Ida into the Scamander near Troy: often in the *Iliad.*

442. **Euboea**: island off east coast of Greece. Aulis, the traditional site of the mustering of the Greek fleet, lies between the island and the mainland.

444. **Golden armour**: in Homer, Achilles inherited armour given as a wedding-present to Peleus by the gods. While Achilles was sulking and refusing to fight Patroclus borrowed the armour, and Hector killed him and secured it. Thetis had fresh armour made by Hephaestus, the smith-god, which is described in detail. Euripides' description is not identical. He is using another tradition by which Hephaestus made the original armour. The carrying of the arms by Thetis and the nymphs is frequently portrayed on vases.

445-6. **Pelion...Ossa**: mountains of Thessaly, where Achilles grew up. He was tutored by the wise centaur Chiron, an episode finely told by Matthew Arnold in *Empedocles on Etna*. There was another story that Thetis sent Achilles to Scyros to be brought up disguised as a girl to keep him from the war. Euripides uses the story elsewhere: not here. There is a most peculiar effect in the Greek at this point - seven consecutive words with the same ending, something like 'colossal Ossa's mossy fosses across rosy goddesses' haunts'.

449-51. the young runner: see on 439.

Grandson of the salt sea: Thetis, mother of Achilles, was daughter to Nereus, the 'Old Man of the Sea'.

the sons of Atreus: Agamemnon, the commander of the army, Electra's father, and Menelaus, Helen's wronged husband.

the old Centaur: Chiron: see on 445-6.

452. a man from Troy: a prisoner-of-war.

453. Nauplia: the port of Argos on the other side of the bay.

459. Perseus: son of Zeus and Danae, exposed in a floating chest and rescued. When he grew up he was sent to get the head of the Gorgon Medusa, a monster whose glance turned all to stone. This he did with the help of a reflecting shield from Athene (so that he need not look directly), a cap of invisibility from the nymphs, a sword from Hermes, and winged shoes from Hermes or the nymphs. Aeschylus had already drawn a parallel between him and Orestes *(Choephoroe* 832).

462-3. Hermes: well-described as the god of country places. Most scholars think him the personification of the cairn, which guides one's steps in mountainous country. He was naturally the god of shepherds, of travellers, of bandits, the messenger of the gods: he even escorted souls on their hazardous journey to the underworld. He was a god of serendipity and good luck. His statue or 'herm', an oblong pillar with head and erect phallus, stood in the streets of Athens, and it was an ill omen when drunken aristocrats in 415 knocked off the symbols of fertility. His mother Maia was one of the Pleiads, and bore Hermes to Zeus.

468. The Pleiads and the Hyades: constellations, in mythology daughters of Atlas and the Ocean nymph Pleione. The five Hyades ('Rainers') were made stars in reward for nursing Dionysus, or in grief for their brother Hyas. The seven Pleiads killed themselves in grief for their sisters, and joined them in the sky, or were made stars to save them from Orion.

Hector: the Trojan hero killed by Achilles in revenge for the death of his friend Patroclus.

471. **Sphinxes**: a monster, part woman and part lion, with wings, emanating from Egypt, who devastated Thebes in the Oedipus-saga. Her riddles were in verse ('enchantments' in the translation). The Sphinx had a curious fascination for the Greeks, and often appears in vase-painting and sculpture.

473. **lioness breathing fire**: another monster, the chimaera, with the forequarters of a lioness, middle of a she-goat, and snake's tail, overcome by another hero Bellerophon. What is the point of all these references to monsters? Who are the monsters - Clytemnestra and Aegisthus? Or Electra and Orestes?

475. **Pegasus the horse of Pyrene**: winged horse, caught by Bellerophon while drinking from the spring of Peirene (Pyrene is a misprint) at Corinth, and his ally in his adventures. Pegasus was born of the dying Medusa's blood (see on 459).

480. **daughter of Tyndareus**: Clytemnestra. But Helen, the overt cause of the Trojan War, was also daughter of Tyndareus, and she sent the warriors to their death.

485. **The day will come**: a sinister phrase. The whole song is filled with the monstrous, and one imagines an accompanying dance of much ugliness.

487-698. *Second Episode. An old man appears and identifies Orestes to Electra. The scene is broken by a brief song of joy from the chorus. The three plan revenge and offer prayer.*

487. **Where's...Where's**: he is excited. The old man is delightfully portrayed.

489. **up to her house**: an indication of a few steps up to a raised stage.

497. **Dionysus' treasure**: wine.

501. **my old coat**: see on 185.

510. **I was alone**: Aegisthus has banned care of the tomb: the loyal old man had not previously dared to break this, and now has done so only unobserved.

512. **myrtle-branches**: the myrtle was a sacred tree, especially but not solely associated with Aphrodite, and easy to make into wreaths.

518. **Perhaps - perhaps**: a very cautious suggestion.

525. **would have come here secretly**: exactly what he did.

527. **the two locks correspond**: recognition-scenes were part of the stock-in-trade of Greek tragedy. Aristotle *(Poetics* 16,1) says that the use of 'tokens' is the least artistic form of recognition. This

would include Aeschylus' three signs, and Euripides' use of the scar. He also says that there is special power in the coincidence of the Recognition and Reversal. Reversal *(peripeteia)* is not just the change of fortune, whether from prosperity to adversity or adversity to prosperity, but a change in which the agent is hoping for the opposite effect. This play provides a subtle example. Orestes and Electra expect their reunion to bring prosperity - but does it?

Euripides is writing in deliberate criticism of the famous recognition-scene in Aeschylus *Choephoroe*. There three signs 'prove' the identity. The first is the lock of hair: brothers and sisters do not have identical hair. The second is the footprint: still less do they have identical footprints. The third is the cloak: it will not be still in use on a grown man. In the scar Euripides invents a recognition-device (borrowed from *The Odyssey*) far more plausible, and no doubt received, or hoped for, an outburst of applause.

528. **palaestra**: hall for wrestling, a regular form of exercise. The parallel between Orestes and the athlete Achilles is important.

529. **Softened with combing**: her hair is not totally uncared-for (184)!

532. **shoe-prints**: the second sign.

539. **cloak**: the third sign.

549. **Here they come**: indicative of the stage direction.

553. **Electra**: a subtle dramatic touch. A new acquaintance would not so address her. Orestes momentarily forgets himself.

559. **a new silver coin**: a forged coin will be new-minted.

565-6. **God...gods**: the Greeks moved freely between both forms of religious expression. Monotheism and polytheism are not always totally incompatible. A single divine power may take more than one form. Many religions believe in a single High God with ministers: Zeus came to fulfil some such role.

573. **This scar**: the clinching evidence. It is pointed by giving the old man two lines breaking into the line-for-line exchange to this point.

579. **At last I hold you close**: they break into half-lines as their emotions tumble out.

582. **And if I catch**: an obvious enough but vivid metaphor.

585. **It has come**: the Chorus has a *hyporchema* or song of joy accompanied by a vigorous dance. *Hyporchema* is a term hard to

61

define precisely. It seems to have started in Crete, as a combination of instrumental music, song, dance and pantomime. It was used in honour of Zeus, Apollo and Dionysus, and in the last capacity found its way into tragedy.

600. **And on my mother**: some scholars think this line a later insertion, partly because the Greek does not scan, and partly because Orestes does not elsewhere at this point speak openly of matricide.

602. **bankrupt**: Euripides is rich in metaphors.

612. **Yes, that's my aim**: this line initiates over 70 lines of *stichomythia* (see on 220) broken only at 651-2, where Electra has a couplet.

625. **The Nymphs**: spiritual powers of the countryside, of trees and shrubs, springs and streams, and mountains. Much of ancient Greek religion had to do with the propitiation of such powers. All nature was numinous, filled with power. It is hard to know whether there is a special point: the Naiads, for instance, granted fertility. Perhaps he was just protecting his pastureland. The Nymphs would be strange recipients of the actual prayer 805-7, though this might have been added.

630. **who would recognize me**: the timorous hero!

637. **invite you**: the old man, for all his hostility, does not doubt Aegisthus' hospitableness.

638. **unwelcome guest**: Orestes does not care about host-guest relations.

640. **Where is my mother?**: hard to say whether this is an attempt at a complete plan to kill both guilty people, or a sudden note of apprehension.

647. **The killing**: Electra's obsession leads her to break across this dialogue. Greek tragedy, although allowing three speaking actors, seldom has genuine scenes for three characters. They nearly always break into a succession of confrontations for two. Here a very brief exchange between Orestes and Electra enables her to take his place in dialogue with the old man.

651-2. **This: go and tell her**: two lines in the Greek, breaking through the *stichomythia,* and therefore unusually powerful.

652. **a son**: verisimilitude? So that she may fear an avenger? To make greater the contrast between the desired male and the low estate?

654. **Ten days ago**: the time for the naming-ceremony: in much of

Africa it is eight days. The blood of childbirth was deemed to lead to uncleanness, and the need of purification; perhaps too in such an awesome moment there is a sense of a need to be sure that the mother is free from the relics of contact with whatever world the new life has come from: she too needs a *rite de passage.* Ceremonies for purification after childbirth are spelt out in *Leviticus.* The churching of women is a recognized Christian ceremony. The *amphidromia* was an Athenian festival in which the child was carried round the hearth. The Greeks counted inclusively, so the natural English is 'Nine days ago'.

655. **And how**: the old man is startled and sceptical.

656. **she will come**: Electra understands her mother's psychology - all too well.

671-82. **Zeus...!**: these twelve lines form a real and powerfully dramatic scene for three: see on 647. Zeus is invoked as Patroos, ancestral god of the family, and Tropaios, Router (of the Trojans for Agamemnon and hopefully of his surviving enemies).

672. **Have pity on us**: Electra reverts to self-pity.

674. **Hera**: see on 172, 174. But Hera helped in childbirth and they have just honoured her with a lie.

675. **If these our prayers are just**: strong irony.

677. **My father**: it is bold to invoke the spirit of the dead hero in conjunction with the two great deities of Olympus. The direction of prayer is changed from sky to ground.

678. **my beating hands**: she strikes the earth as she speaks.

682. **Father, so outraged by my mother**: Electra continues to strike the ground: her fanaticism continues after the others have done. She is as motivated by hatred of her mother as by love of her father.

685. **this token-word**: what does this mean? Some scholars think that Electra does not rise, but that she is still speaking to Agamemnon, urging his support, and there is much to be said for this view. Others hold that she is speaking a word of good omen to the murderers, or that she is proposing a kind of password.

694. **in both hands**: they go out to audience-left (to the country).

699-746. *Second Stasimon.*

699. **Long ago**: Electra goes into the house.

This choral dance and song is in two pairs of matching stanzas without final epode. It places the present events in their mythical context: see on 432. For the myth see intr. sect. 12. This golden-fleeced lamb has nothing to do with the more famous golden fleece of Jason's quest. The choral song covers an indefinite length of time in the action. As with the previous song this is a masterpiece in the brutalization of beauty, turning to adultery, deceit and theft, and, beyond, murder and cannibalism. We can only regret the loss of music and choreography.

703. **Pan**: awesome god of the wildwood and pastures, who causes pan-ic.

716. **The flute, servant of the Muses**: not however played transversely, but more like our recorder or clarinet. The flute is personified: usually the poet is servant of the Muses. The Muses were nine sisters, daughters of Zeus and Memory; they presided over all forms of poetry, singing and dancing, as well as history and astronomy. *Mousike* in Greek is far wider than our 'music', and a museum a shrine to the Muses, where historians, poets, scientists and musicians might work, not a monument to the past. See also note on *Medea* 1031-2.

. 734. **the parched plains of Ammon**: the western desert of Egypt. Ammon was a ram-headed oracle-god identified with Zeus.

737. **But I can hardly believe**: Euripides indulges in a spot of rationalism, not specially appropriate to the chorus.

743. **frightening tales are useful**: so a character in a satyr-play *(Sisyphus)* by Critias put forward the view that all religion is an artificial bastion for morality.

745. **Had you but remembered**: the apparent irrelevance is made dramatically apposite. Why did she not remember them? Why does not Orestes now not remember them?

747-1146. *Third Episode. A messenger arrives with news of Aegisthus' death. There is a brief choral interlude (859-879). Electra shows her hatred of the dead Aegisthus and her determination to kill her mother. Orestes draws back. Clytemnestra arrives and debates with Electra.*

747. **Ah!**: very dramatic. Just as we expect the epode, a spoken cry breaks off the song and arrests us.

749. **The gale is up**: metaphorical or literal? If literal, then 'There's enough wind to bring the sound of the assassination.' If metaphorical, 'The breeze of Fortune is rising.'

750. **Come out here!**: the indication that she has not been present during the choral ode.

755. **an Argive voice**: belonging to either Aegisthus or Orestes.

64

766. I'm your brother's servant!: the speaking actor is wearing the mask and costume of one of those walking-on parts addressed at 360.

774. After we left the cottage: the beginning of a dramatic speech 85 lines long. Although drama is essentially something *done* or *acted,* not *narrated,* it was a convention that a climactic episode, often violent and sometimes impossible of portrayal on stage, should not be shown on stage but described in a rhetorical showpiece by a messenger.

776. the great king of Mycenae: stock form of title.

778. myrtle-leaves: slightly curious, in that myrtle was especially sacred to Aphrodite, goddess of love. See also on 512.

781. Thessalians: from the great riverplain and mountain uplands of north-east Greece, which bred Achilles.

Alpheius: river of Elis by the great sanctuary of Olympia.

784. Must share the banquet: meat was a luxury in the ancient world, and a sacrifice was a rare occasion for enjoying meat.

793. We have purified ourselves: if he had taken part in the purification ceremony with Aegisthus the murder would have been too great a sacrilege even for him. Denniston has an excellent summary of sacrificial ritual: see Homer *The Odyssey* 3,230-65; Aristophanes *Peace* 939ff.; Euripides *Iphigeneia in Aulis* 1467-1569. First the victim was garlanded. Then barleymeal, wreath and the knife of sacrifice were placed in a basket and carried round the altar, which stood in front of the temple (if any) in the open air. The sacrificer took a piece of burning wood from the altar-fire, dipped it in a bowl of lustral water and with it sprinkled altar, victim and congregation, thereby dedicating the victim to death. The barleymeal was sprinkled on the altar-fire and on the victim's head. The sacrificer cut a tuft of hair from the victim and placed it on the fire, another act of dedication to death. At some point in these proceedings the sacrificer prayed aloud with congregational participation. Finally with flutes sounding the victim's throat was cut, the blood flowing into the sacrificial bowl, the tongue was cut out, and the body flayed and carved. Some portions were reserved to the gods, and the rest consumed by the congregation: a myth told how the trickster-god Prometheus conned Zeus into accepting a larger package comprising the less palatable objects rather than a smaller one of the good meat. Certain aspects of the internal organs would tell whether the sacrifice was well-omened and accepted.

795. **if strangers**: the true heir to the throne speaks with irony.

798-9. **laid by their spears**: so that the trusting king was defenceless.

807. **my enemies**: the messenger identifies these with Electra and Orestes: but it is a standard prayer for the safety of the state.

819. **Dorian sword**: presumably one with a sharp blade.

823. **a fast runner**: the theme of athletics: see on 439, 528.

827. **The liver-lobe was missing...**: items of ill omen.

834. **a Phthian sword**: heavier, for the murder. Phthia is in Thessaly.

839. **bending over them**: the heroic Orestes strikes him down from behind.

856. **no Gorgon's head**: the glance of the Gorgon Medusa turned people to stone. Perseus killed her by always looking in the mirror of his polished shield, not directly, and used the head to petrify (literally) his enemies. A key theme; cf. 459.

859. **Oh, Electra!**: a brief choral dance and song of joy in two matching stanzas separated by spoken words from Electra.

860. **like a light fawn**: a lovely image, perhaps taken from the lyric poet Bacchylides, 13,84-90, more appropriate than that of the nineteenth-century cleric who prayed that Queen Victoria might 'dance like a he-goat on the mountains'.

871. **I must bring out**: equivalent to the following stage-direction.

875. **to delight the Muses**: see on 716.

880-1. **worthy son of him who conquered Troy**: Comparisons are dangerous if they involve contrasts, and the contrast between the defeat of the heroic Trojans and the stabbing of a defenceless man in the back is deliberately invoked by the playwright. A fine visual scene as she garlands him: but the glory will fade faster than the flowers.

883. **run your full course**: a good image. A Greek race was run there-and-back. Orestes has been out to Phthia and returned successfully. It reinforces the image of the athlete: 439, 528, 823.

896. **throw out his carcase**: after Orestes' pious words, an extraordinary violation of the Greek view of divine law, which required the burial of the enemy, no matter what he had done. See on 289.

907. **Of all the harsh and bitter things**: this speech of vicious hatred is without parallel in Greek tragedy, and can be compared only with the lyric poet Archilochus (probably seventh century

B.C.) at his most intransigent. The real Electra bursts out.

What shall come first...: a standard rhetorical division.

917. **never saw Troy**: the contrast between Agamemnon's military gallantry and Aegisthus' cowardice is a commonplace of the tradition.

919. **find a faithful wife**: there is nothing else in the tradition to suggest that Clytemnestra was not loyal to Aegisthus; therefore this is an example of Electra's diseased imaginings.

931. **'Clytemnestra's husband'**: Athenian males would join in shaking their heads at such an idea. But it is a curious sequence of crimes - adultery, murder, cowardice, complaisance - and letting his wife 'wear the trousers'. It comes oddly from Electra, who domineers over her brother. But Electra has a father-fixation.

936. **above his station**: by birth Aegisthus was as noble as Agamemnon: she denigrates him.

939. **great wealth**: he took over Agamemnon's; his exiled father Thyestes (see intr. sect. 12) will have lost most of his. Sententious expressions, like those which follow, were popular with Greek audiences. But these reflect a change from the time when *arete* (excellence, social effectiveness) included wealth as a necessary part to an age when it is coming to mean moral virtue. See J. Ferguson *Moral Values in the Ancient World* pp. 19-21; A. W. H. Adkins *Merit and Responsibility* passim.

945. **virgin**: she remains bitter about this.

947-9. **good looks, indulged...girl-faced fop**: this is Euripides' invention - or Electra's.

948. **Give me for a husband**: she has one, and he is not a girl-faced fop but a true man: but he does not count in her mind.

953. **Let no man**: more sententiousness. This is the commonplace 'Call no one happy till he is dead', as in the alleged dialogue between Solon and Croesus (Herodotus 1,32): Croesus, the millionaire king of Lydia, expected to be called the happiest man alive, but received Solon's warning. But the athletics image transfers it from Aegisthus to Orestes: see on 883.

957-8. **His crimes...**: the Chorus tends to make a 'balanced' comment after a long speech.

959-61. **Men...throat is cut**: decisive and bloodthirsty.

962-3. **What is it?...my mother**: equivalent to a stage-direction.

965-6. **Good...gown**: full of bitter spite.

967. **What shall we do, then?**: Orestes weakens.

968. **Have you grown soft?...**: Electra hardens. Throughout the dialogue the contrast in characterization is brilliant.

971. **Phoebus, your oracle**: the first questioning of its authority, a moment of powerful drama.

975. **Avenging him...; but killing her...**: this is the moral dilemma.

979. **Some fiend**: a startling improbability, though later there was a stronger belief in the power of evil spirits to usurp the powers of the good, appearing in deceptive guises.

985. **I'll go in**: stage direction.

988. **Daughter of Tyndareos**: the Chorus greet Clytemnestra in anapaests (♩♩♩), a rhythm often used for entrances. It has been suggested that their fulsome greeting is designed to create in her the sort of pride which will call down the anger of the gods.

990-1. **the two noble sons of Zeus**: Castor and Polydeuces (Pollux), also born to Zeus and Leda with their two sisters, known as the Dioscuri or Dioscori. They were identified with the twin lights of St. Elmo's fire, and with the constellation Gemini. There was a strong belief about this time in the identification of the stars with spiritual powers: Plato gave philosophical expression to it. The fiery heaven refers to the *aether*. Many Greek thinkers regarded the material world as a globe, with outside it the infinite divine mind-stuff, which permeated to the highest parts, forming the fiery upper air or *aether*. Hence in Aristophanes' play *The Clouds,* Socrates is 'discovered' in a basket, feeding his mind on the *aether*.

992. **honoured on stormy seas**: their appearance as St. Elmo's fire on ships' masts was a factor in their position as protectors of sailors from storm.

994. **as one of the blessed gods**: to the Greeks this was blasphemy: Alexander the Great caused a great deal of scandal when he demanded to be worshipped.

998. **Get out of the carriage, Trojan slaves**: another equivalent to a series of stage directions affecting her entrance. The emphasis on Troy reminds us of Agamemnon's victory.

1002. **the child I lost**: Iphigeneia (intr. sect. 12). This turns us to sympathy towards her.

1006. **royal hand**: the word, rightly translated for its implications, means literally something like 'blessed', and is strongly ironical in view of Clytemnestra's imminent death.

1008. **prisoner by the sword**: Electra overdramatizes herself.

1011ff. **Your father, child**: a formal *agon*, contest or debate, between mother and daughter starts here, dramatically strong and appropriate. Clytemnestra presents a good case, and appears gentle and reasonable. She makes two points: the murder of Iphigeneia (intr. sect. 12) and the introduction of Cassandra as a concubine, implying (untruly) that this preceded her liaison with Aegisthus. But her attack on the twofold standard of morality by which men sow their wild oats while women become culpably damaged goods is unanswered.

1019. **To die**: i.e. if he killed his daughter he was capable of killing his wife.

1020. **with lies about Achilles**: Iphigeneia was to marry Achilles.

1022. **Aulis**: between Euboea and mainland Greece, a well-protected harbour.

held her high: finely portrayed in a painting in the House of the Tragic Poet in Pompeii.

1037. **She'll copy him**: the implication that Agamemnon's behaviour over Cassandra preceded her adultery with Aegisthus is untrue. But she could be implying something wider about character. After all, *The Iliad* starts when Agamemnon has to give up Chryseis 'whom I prefer to my wife Clytemnestra' (Homer *The Iliad* 1,113) and takes instead Briseis, Achilles' girl.

1040. **The husbands are to blame - but they're not criticized**: a challenge to established values.

1041. **Suppose Menelaus**: no doubt the males in the audience gave this a sarcastic laugh, but she is making a real point, which involves stereotypes of male and female.

1051-4. **Your words are just**: the Chorus takes a balanced view, leaning to the side of conventional wisdom. The idea that justice may be repellent or shameful is, however, bold. It is an ironical preparation for the shameful justice to be inflicted by Orestes and Electra.

1060. **I'll say it, then**: as Denniston says, Electra cannot resist this bitter attack on her mother, even though she is risking sending her off in a fury and so spoiling their plans. It is noteworthy that she attacks her mother to her living face: with Aegisthus she waited till he was dead.

1066. **the most noble man in Hellas**: her idealization of her father is a trait in her character.

1072. **A wife who in her husband's absence**: centuries later Clement of Alexandria, writing for Christians, permits a woman whose husband has a roving eye to use make-up to attract him back - but not for anyone else.

1082. **whom Hellas chose**: his claim to the throne of Argos was hereditary. But he was elected from among the kings to command the expeditionary force.

1086. **your daughter**: but also his daughter.   Electra turns Clytemnestra's motive to personal grievance alone.

1090. **bought yourself a husband**: forgetting that she has just been commenting on her mother's beauty.

1092. **Nor death for mine**: dramatic irony, since he does suffer death.   Electra exaggerates the wrongs he suffers, seeing them as worse than her brother's.

1093-4. **if death in justice demands death**: so a blood-feud has no end; so violence provokes counter-violence and escalates - still today.

1096. **so is the other**: five lines follow in the Greek (three from Electra and two from the chorus) which are omitted as an interpolation, the three coming from another play.

1102. **My child**: Clytemnestra remains patient and forgiving.   A daughter's fixation for her father and consequent hostility to her mother is called an Electra-complex.   The Greek word for 'love' has overtones of 'be indulgent to'.

1109-10. **How bitterly I regret it now!**: there is no reason to treat this as insincere.   It is in marked contrast with Clytemnestra in Sophocles *Electra* (549) 'I have no misgivings at what has passed.'

1116. **Aegisthus**: lit. 'your husband', a bitter expression.

1120. **He lives in my house**: not 'lives' but 'resides'.   There is an ironical double meaning: overtly 'He has usurped the palace', covertly 'He is dead in the cottage'.

1121. **kindling**: lit. 'bringing to life', which she cannot do.

1122. **I'm afraid of him - so much afraid**: lit. 'I fear him - as I fear him', ambiguously.

1126. **tenth-day sacrifice**: see on 654.

1131. **we don't have friends**: she overdramatizes herself as usual: they are no worse off than other peasant farmers.

1132. **I'll go in**: the translator has spoiled the dramatic impact a little by bringing forward the words 'as a favour'.   Clytemnestra's

70

generous compassion to the daughter who has flayed her with her tongue seals her doom.

1139. **Please come in**: exaggerated courtesy. Electra is bitter about the upper-class clothes she is deprived of wearing (and adds to the bitterness by wearing filthy rags instead of decent working-class clothes). But it is not the smoky wall which will soil the dress.

1141. **The sacrifice that is due**: ironical double meaning.

1143. **the bull**: Aegisthus. The sacrificial victim and symbol of male sexual prowess.

1147-71. *Final Stasimon, broken by death-cries of Clytemnestra.*

1147. **Now retribution follows sin**: this translation misses the ambiguity, since the words mean something like 'One evil is exchanged for another'. The chorus in these two matching stanzas of song and dance certainly come down on the side of the young murderers - but not for long, and the opening words are ominously ambiguous.

1148. **a new wind blows**: a natural metaphor to a nation of seafarers.

by the water of purification: he was killed in his bath.

1155. **like a returning tide**: not quite, as the Mediterranean has next to no tide. But changing current is familiar enough in the strait between Euboea and the mainland near Aulis.

1158. **Cyclopean**: the Cyclopes were one-eyed giant smiths and masons who built the massive walls of Mycenae. Such architecture today bears the name 'Cyclopean'.

1162. **lioness**: a vivid simile taken from Aeschylus *(Agamemnon* 1258), but going further, for this lioness has lost her young.

1165. **My children**: Clytemnestra's last words, except for her death-cry, are a plea for pity.

1172-1359. *Exodos. The bodies are brought out, the murderers now disorientated sing. The Dioscuri, brothers of Clytemnestra, appear, condemn the revenge, however merited, and foretell what is to come. Brother and sister part.*

1174. **trophy of triumph**: a military metaphor - but the victory is not over a mighty military power but over a beseeching cry.

1176. **Tantalus**: see intr. sect. 12.

1177. **O Earth!**: although there is no indication of it, it is likely that the body was brought out on the wheeled platform or *ekkyklema* (intr. sect. 2), forming a tableau with Orestes and Electra, who then step down. A song follows in three pairs of matching stanzas (1177-89 = 1190-1205; 1206-12 = 1214-20; 1221-6 = 1227-32). Some lines are missing from the first stanza. The first and last pair are shared between Orestes, Electra and the chorus; in the central pair Orestes and Electra are in turn answered by the chorus. It should be a song of triumph: it is in fact a song of misery, guilt and degradation. Earth is the primal mother-goddess, Zeus the power of the overarching sky. The chorus moves to a general condemnation of the murder, though with some uncertainty.

1182. **I am guilty**: Electra does not try to hide behind the oracle.

1186. **Mother of curses!**: her children were a curse to her.

1190. **O Phoebus**: Apollo, the god of the Delphic oracle. Oracular commands are often ambiguous: this comes close to calling them unjust, for the suggestion is that the apparent justice of retribution was no justice at all.

1194. **To what city**: in *Iphigeneia among the Taurians* the foreign king Thoas is appalled at the matricide.

1199-1200. **accept me as his wife**: the worthy peasant is forgotten: she fears she is to live up to her name Electra, 'unwedded'.

1205. **Forcing him against his will**: she is the dominant partner, her mother's daughter.

1207. **thrust forth her breast**: part of the tradition: they are not turned aside by the breasts that suckled them. Clytemnestra need not be thought of as an old lady: she could have been in her late thirties.

1211. **shriek**: the Greek is very subtle, describing her cry as 'grievous', but with overtones of a cry to Apollo, and a cry for healing.

1221. **I held my cloak over my eyes**: as Perseus did not look at the Gorgon (459).

1222. **performed sacrifice**: he uses a ritual word to direct his own thought from what he was really doing.

1233. **Shining above the house**: on the theologeion (intr. sect. 2). The words are a stage direction for their appearance, but do not identify them: they do this themselves at 1239-40. See on 990-1. The last scene is played on three levels - good visual drama.

1238. **Listen, son of Agamemnon!**: Castor does the speaking,

72

and appears in character as a bluff, no-nonsense sailor.

1244. **Her fate was just: but your act is not justified**: this is a major theme of tragedy - and history: human beings try to act as gods.

1245. **he is my lord**: the Dioscori are minor deities, Apollo a major one; but the silence is an eloquent condemnation, made overt enough later (1266, 1296-7, 1302). The condemnation raises questions about Euripides' theology. In *Hippolytus* Aphrodite and Artemis seem to represent the powers of Passion and Chastity; to ignore either may be disastrous. In *The Bacchae* Dionysus is the power of religious ecstasy. But what of Apollo? In this context Apollo is the Delphic Oracle, and that had all too human manipulators, not just in mythical antiquity but in the fifth century.

1248. **Fate and Zeus**: here coupled, but there are passages in Greek literature where Zeus is subordinate to Fate (lit. one's share): Homer *The Iliad* 16,440-2; 22,179-80; Aeschylus *Prometheus* 515-9.

1249. **give Electra to Pylades**: part of the tradition, but one wonders what he has done to deserve such a fate.

1252. **those dread Fates**: it is a mistake to repeat the word 'Fate'; these are totally different powers of death and destruction.

the dog-faced Goddesses: the Erinyes or Furies, identified with the powers of death. In Aeschylus *Oresteia* they are like hounds on the trail of the guilty. They had snakes in their hair (1256), and pick up the Gorgon motif.

1254. **holy image**: not Pheidias' work of gold and ivory, but the ancient wooden image.

1257. **the circle of her Gorgon-shield**: the *aegis*, possessed by Zeus and Athene for power and protection. It seems to have been originally a stormcloud, but a false derivation made it a goatskin, sometimes held over the left arm like a shield. Athene's had an edging of snakes and a Gorgon's head in the middle. The Gorgon was a monster, snake-haired with eyes that petrified: the symbol of the head had great apotropaic power (i.e. averting evil).

1258. **Hill of Ares**: the Areopagus at the foot of the Acropolis, above the agora or city-centre. Ares was the Greek war-god.

1259. **the first murder-trial**: Aeschylus dated the formation of the court from the trial of Orestes. Euripides puts it further back, but dates the practice of acquittal *when the votes were equal* to Orestes. The sea-god Poseidon had a son Halirrhothius who raped

73

Alcippe, daughter of Ares. Ares killed Halirrhothius, was indicted by Poseidon and acquitted.

1263. **a court**: originally called 'the Council', then 'the Council of the Areopagus', at first of birthright nobles, from the sixth century or earlier, of ex-archons. In early days it will have been a kind of Privy Council, but its functions became exclusively judicial and religious. After the democratic revolution of 462-1 it lost all political power, but remained the court for murder.

1265-6. **The votes being equal shall acquit you**: this was the tradition, and was supposed to date back to Orestes' trial. It used to be assumed that in Aeschylus *Oresteia* the human judges were equally divided and Athene gave the casting vote for acquittal, but H. D. F. Kitto showed reasons for thinking that Athene was one of the twelve judges, and her vote made things equal and therefore for acquittal.

1266. **Loxias**: Apollo. The name means 'oblique', possibly from his ambiguous oracles, or from the passage of the sun through the ecliptic.

1270. **The dread Goddesses**: see on 1252. In Aeschylus they are persuaded to accept their new role and become the Eumenides or kindly goddesses.

1271. **deep chasm**: in the north-eastern corner of the Areopagus.

1273-5. **Arcadia**: rural mountainous area of the central Peloponnese, dominated by the river Alpheius, and containing a town called Orestheion, whose precise location is uncertain. Zeus Lycaeus was worshipped as a rain god on a mountain in Arcadia, with a tradition of human sacrifice: arguments have been brought to suggest that the title is derived from 'light' or 'wolf'.

1277. **tomb of earth**: an inferior burial. The great traditions of the Mycenaean age were of huge stone-built 'beehive' tombs for the wealthy and honoured, such as may still be seen at Mycenae.

1280. **Helen**: see on 213-4. Nauplia was the other side of the bay from Argos and served as its port (cf. 453).

1281. **Never saw Troy**: Stesichorus, a lyric poet of the sixth century, wrote a poem in which he told the story of Helen's adultery. Legend says that he was struck blind till he recanted, and he may well have offended against public opinion in Sparta where Helen was a divine figure. In the recantation he wrote 'It's all a lie:/you never sailed in the well-benched ships,/never trod the towers of Troy.' Hera, resentful at not receiving the prize from

Paris, baulked him of Aphrodite's bribe (the most beautiful woman in the world) and substituted a breathing likeness fashioned from *aether* or upper air, whisking the real Helen away to Egypt where Proteus was king. This was the theme of Euripides *Helen,* performed in 412, or, just possibly, with *Electra* in 413 (J. Ferguson *A Companion to Greek Tragedy* pp. 412-3). See intr. sect. 11.

1285. **Phocis:** see on 18.

1286. **the peasant:** not in the Greek. It is a good thought that his admirable qualities are recognised.

1288. **The Corinthian Isthmus:** the neck of land, narrowing to about 3.5 miles in width, linking the Peloponnese to the rest of Greece.

1289. **Cecrops:** legendary first king of Athens, said to have invented writing and instituted monogamy and the burial of the dead.
Rock: the Acropolis with its temples.

1290. **the appointed period for blood-guilt:** in classical Athens unintentional homicide involved a year's exile. But in the myth Orestes had first to find acquittal, and then go to the land of the Tauri in the north of the Black Sea, and bring to Greece a holy image of Artemis.

1294. **you are not polluted:** they have addressed the polluted Orestes, but he certainly may not speak without permission.

1300. **Not shield her:** the translator has altered the order of lines in the MSS. The gods have no real answer. The epiphany, good theatre as it is, is no solution. Gods do not intervene to save us from the consequences of our acts. They do not intervene to save the warring states of fifth-century Greece. Euripides uses the epiphany-which-is-no-solution with great power in *Orestes.*

1295. **Sons of Tyndareos:** there is some uncertainty whether Orestes or Electra is speaking.

1297. **Apollo's shoulder:** here they place the responsibility openly on Delphi.

1307. **your fathers:** Tantalus, Pelops, Atreus (intr. sect. 12).

1319. **Pallas:** Athene.

1330. **pity for the suffering of mankind:** a noteworthy sentiment, not always to be found among the Greeks. Of course, the Dioscuri are tinged with humanity; they are not aloof and Olympian.

1342. **avenging hounds:** the Furies: see on 1252.

1347. **Sicily**: this must refer to the relief expedition of 413 to the original Athenian imperialistic expedition of 415. The date of production must be regarded as firm, though suggestions of style indicate that it was written some years before.

1350-1. **blasphemers...goodness**: whether or not a specific reference is intended the audience would pick up a contrast between those responsible for mutilating the statues of Hermes and parodying the Mysteries just before the expedition sailed in 415, and an ultra-religious man such as Nicias (who was none the less doomed to defeat and death).